# WALKING WITH THE KING

## Keswick Ministry

from Alec Motyer, Philip Hacking,
Eric Alexander, Tom Houston, and others

### Edited by David Porter

**STL Books**

PO Box 48, Bromley, Kent, England
PO Box 28, Waynesboro, Georgia, USA
PO Box 656, Bombay 13, India

Keswick Convention Council, England

©1982 The Keswick Convention Council

STL Books are published by Send The Light (Operation Mobilisation),
9 London Road, Bromley, Kent, England.

ISBN 0 903843 65 X

Made and printed by
Hunt Barnard Printing Ltd, Aylesbury, Bucks.

# CONTENTS

# INTRODUCTION

*by Canon A S Neech*
*(Chairman of the Keswick Council)*

In this book are words that deeply moved hundreds of people at Keswick 1982. Difficulties of transport because of a rail strike or the current economic situation seemed to make little or no difference to attendance this year, and the crowds were as great as ever and probably even greater than last year.

Some found the secret of a new life in Jesus Christ. Many discovered with sheer delight how relevant, practical and satisfying the Word of God is. Dozens talked of a new-found joy, or of discovering a new direction for their lives. Hundreds had their faith confirmed and their courage renewed as they yielded afresh to the Lordship of Christ.

Reading an account, or even watching a big occasion televised, can never be quite like being present. The indescribable hush that falls across a crowd of thousands in the big tent as God's Spirit applies the words that are being spoken, the sense of freedom in prayer when God's presence is a real experience, the joy of meeting, sharing and talking with other Christians – all these are 'better felt than tell't'. Nevertheless, through these pages, something of the inspiration of those two great weeks of Convention can become yours as you read these pages; and you will know a little more of the communion of saints as you make your own the great affirmations of the faith expounded here, and make your response to the challenge of God's Word.

Immediate sales of tapes at Keswick are one small indication of the effect of any address. By this criterion, God used every single talk to help some who first heard it given. But printed words have many advantages over every other form of communication; and here you have a book which cannot but be a blessing to you. Keep it for future reference, and buy some more to pass on to friends.

Once more David Porter has had the enjoyable but difficult task of reducing all that is said at Keswick to the limits prescribed by the pages of the book. All of us are grateful for his skill and expertise and the enthusiasm he brings to his work.

# EDITOR'S INTRODUCTION

Sorting through the papers of my late and beloved father, I recently found a much-read copy of the 1946 *Keswick Year*. The War was over, but its shadow still fell across the Convention; 'It seemed almost like a dream,' wrote the Chairman of the Council, 'to be walking again the streets of this little lakeside town.' The message of Keswick – the call to a practical, personal holiness – rang the more clearly because of the horrors that had gone before.

Now, almost half a century later, we live in a different world; but how much remains the same! This year's Keswick Convention took place against the background of horrific international events, of the arrival in London of a man who actually claimed to be the Christ, of grievous blurrings of biblical truth by those whose commission was to proclaim truth, and a general loss of direction in our society. And against that background, the messages of joy and peace contained in this book stand sharply defined.

We have expanded the book this year, and the result is that we have been able to give much more of a 'feel' of the structure of the Convention. Three 'pairs' of addresses are included, which were given after each other at the evening convention meetings. With the extra space we have been able to include more than usual of the inter-relationship between the messages. One of the simplest and most dramatic evidences of God's hand on the Convention is the way in which speakers who have not consulted each other constantly dovetail into each other's themes and concerns. For an example, glance at the opening of Rev Alec Motyer's exposition of Psalm 51 on page 210.

In 1946 all the speakers rewrote their material for publication in the *Keswick Year*. It was a more leisurely age then. In more recent years speakers have graciously waived the right to check their material before publication, so that the book can be published before Christmas (the book is carefully read by a member of the Keswick Council before publication). It is important that readers understand that this material is consequently not to be seen as a polished, revised, 'book' version of the speakers' messages, such as they might have produced at their leisure, but an edited transcript of what was said from the platform. In the spirit of that, we have once more left biblical quotations largely as they were read by the speakers – paraphrase was often used by them to make a point – and I have always assumed that readers will have a Bible open just as the speakers assumed their listeners would in the tent. You can enjoy the book perfectly well without that, but you will get a great deal more from the addresses if you do.

I and the Keswick Council are extremely grateful to the army of typists who worked on initial transcripts of the material. It was a pleasant surprise this year to find several friends and acquaintances among them. The transcribers have all done an excellent job in a wonderful spirit, and many have mentioned that the work was a particular blessing to them. I would certainly add my own testimony to theirs.

Once again, I must remind readers of the excellent tape library, details of which appear on page 256. On the tapes you will find for example the wealth of warm interplay between Philip Hacking and his hearers which your relentless editor has had to prune; you will hear for example the inimitable delivery of Ronald Dunn, which no written words could capture; and you will hear all the usual anecdotes and jokes (the jokes this year reached a remarkably high standard!) which had to go so that as much as possible of the teaching could be included.

*David Porter*

# THE BIBLE READINGS

# SON OF DAVID, SON OF GOD: MARK 10-16

*by Rev Alec Motyer*

## 1. The King's Unsatisfied Hunger (Mark 10:46-12:40)

May I remind you, as we start, of what John says at the end of his Gospel? If all the things that the Lord Jesus said and did were recorded, 'even the world itself would not contain the books that should be written'. It means, if we take it seriously, that everything we have in each Gospel is there by selection, not because it's the only thing that happened but because it expresses a truth concerning the Lord Jesus which that Gospel-writer desired to express, and which nothing else would express quite so well. They all selected from a mass of material to bring us that wonderful four-fold picture of our Lord Jesus which the Gospels contain. So as we read this passage in Mark, everything is here by design; written for our learning, selected by the writer under the inspiration of the Holy Spirit.

Mark opens this passage with the account of the granting of sight to Bartimaeus. He goes on to tell us, at the beginning of chapter 11, how Jesus rode into Jerusalem upon a donkey. These things happened, of course, but Mark selected them out of many other things that happened in order to get the portrait of Jesus he wanted to share with us. Jesus observes the fig tree: cleanses the temple: returns (verse 20) to the fig tree, finds it withered

up, and teaches – not, as you might have expected, about
the fig tree, but about believing prayer. I believe that, more
than anything else almost, is there by deliberate selection.

Then our passage goes speeding on its way. In verse 27
we read that representatives of the three constituent parties
of the ruling body of the church of His day – the Sanhedrin
– 'came to Him'. In 12:13, the Pharisees, the religious
people, the political compromisers, they came to Him; in
12:18 the Sadducees, the doctrinal liberals, came to speak
to Jesus and to try to puzzle Him with their hard questions.
And finally in 12:28 the scribes came, the orthodox
theologians who spent their days pondering the mysteries
of God; they came to Him. And all the time (verse 37), 'the
common people heard Him gladly'. So the whole of the
people of God at that time are brought into the royal
presence of the Lord Jesus Christ.

### The giving of sight to Bartimaeus (10:46 ff)

The first of these deliberately-recorded incidents is the
second miracle of giving sight. Mark's is a very sparing
Gospel. He only tells us of two of the people to whom the
Lord gave sight. On each occasion he puts the story in with
great accuracy, not just to tell you about something
wonderful that Jesus did, but also to tell you something
wonderful about Jesus Himself; that He is the eye-opening
Lord. Just as He left neither of these people in physical
blindness, so neither will He leave His people alone until
He has imparted a true spiritual sight and understanding.

It would be worthwhile to glance at the other eye-
opening incident in Mark 8:22. When first Jesus laid hands
upon the blind man of Bethsaida, he looked up and saw
men 'as trees, walking'. Then 'again He laid His hands
upon his eyes; and he looked steadfastly, and was restored,
and saw all things clearly' (8:25). Here is a Lord who will
not leave the work unfinished, but will bring His people
through to a full and clear sight and understanding.

On one side of that incident there is blindness, and on the other, a full understanding. The blindness is in 8:21: 'He said to them, do you not yet understand?' See now what happens on the other side of the story. In Mark 8:29 He asks the people to whom He has only recently said, 'Do you not yet understand?', 'Who say you that I am?' Peter speaks for all: 'Thou art the Christ.'

Do you see what I mean, that the story is put deliberately into place? What is the link, between the blindness that doesn't understand, and the clarity that sees Jesus as the Messiah of God? It is the miracle-working Lord.

And in chapter 10 there is on the one side blindness; and – please God, for all of us – on the other side, clarity of vision. The blindness is in 10:35ff: '. . . and they said, Grant unto us that we may sit, one on your right, and one on your left, in your glory.' Matthew is even more blunt; he brings the mother of Zebedee, and she asks outright that they may sit one on His right and one on His left in His kingdom. But the two lads are only interested in the glory; their eyes are dazzled by the glory of the kingdom, but they are thinking of it in earthly terms. They are thinking of a throne of David in Jerusalem with Prime Ministers on this side and that. They are thinking of a kingdom in which Jesus is not interested: 'My kingdom is not of this world.'

How is that blindness, that lack of spiritual vision to be lifted? Look what He can do, says Mark. There was a man named Bartimaeus, and he acclaimed the king, and he saw the king, and he followed the king. He didn't cry out in the name that was mentioned to him, Jesus of Nazareth; he cried out in the name that was meaningful to him, 'Jesus, Thou Son of David'. He acclaimed the king arriving in the royal city; Jesus brought him into His presence and restored his sight, so that he saw the king; and then he followed the king. Mark stresses discipleship; he tells us that when Jesus left Jericho His disciples were round Him. When the man's eyes were opened, he 'followed Him in the way'. And we must follow along with Bartimaeus, so that we may have a clear sight of who this king is and what it means to belong to His kingdom.


## The arrival of the king in the great city (11:1 ff)

Mark is most insistent that this is a king who is coming. In 10:48, 49, Jesus is the prayer-answering king. The beggar hadn't been a life-long beggar for nothing. Shouting was the one thing he knew about. 'And Jesus stood still.' Look at Psalm 72:13 – it's most interesting how Mark sweeps through the old covenant scriptures so that we may have no doubt in our minds that Jesus comes as king. Predictively, of the royal Messiah: 'He shall deliver the needy when he cries, the poor who has no helper.' How true that was of Bartimaeus! He had no one to help him – but the king who hears prayer was there. In Mark 10:52 we find that the sight-giving king is here. Look at Isaiah 35:6, in that marvellous passage about the home-coming of the people of God into the royal city: 'Then the eyes of the blind shall be opened.'

Chapter 11:1-7; did you ever ask yourself why such an inordinate amount of time was spent choosing this donkey? Seven whole verses – far more about the donkey than about the ride! I suggest to you that part of the reason is to be found in Genesis 49:10, 11. You see there a picture of a king on his throne, and his staff – the symbol of his executive royal authority – is resting on his shoulder; and the end of the staff is between his feet. It will not depart 'until Shiloh come'. The only other Old Testament reference to Genesis 10:49 interprets Shiloh as 'he whose right it is'. The rule will remain in the tribe of Judah, until the Judaic ruler shall come whose right it is to reign. One of the signs of his messianic presence (verse 11) is that he binds 'his foal unto the vine, and his ass's colt unto the choice vine'. Now if you were a vineyard-keeper, the last thing you would do would be to tie a donkey to a precious vine. If you can use your vine as a tying-up post, then you are prosperous indeed! And when the king comes, whose right it is to reign, He will bring prosperity with Him, He will bring all the messianic bounty to His people.

Verse 7: they brought the colt to Jesus. And 'many spread their garments upon the way' (verse 8), and 'they that went before, and they that followed, cried, Hosanna . . .' (verse 9); the New Testament reaches back to Zechariah in the Old Testament, Zechariah 9:9, 'Behold thy king cometh unto thee: He is just, and having salvation; lowly, and riding upon an ass . . .'

'He entered Jerusalem, into the temple' (verse 11). Mark isn't interested in anything that happened in the city; he's only interested in the temple. Jesus looked around . . . He saw everything . . . He went out again! Anti-climax! Next day (verse 15) he returned to the temple, to cast out the traders. So was fulfilled that extra part that Malachi, among others, tells us about: 'The Lord shall suddenly come to His temple'. With what dramatic suddenness the king came! He came as king, and He came as God.

But He also came . . . hungry (verse 12). I suppose He had spent the night sleeping rough. 'And seeing a fig tree afar off . . . He came, if haply he might find anything thereon; and when He came to it, He found nothing but leaves.' Commentators tell me that if you see a fig tree in leaf, you can expect to find figs, especially if the fig harvest has not taken place, as was the case here: 'it was not the season of figs' (in 12:2 we will see that the word 'season' is used of the harvesting season). He saw the leaves; in the nature and times of things He expected to find fruit. But contrary to nature and time, He found the fig tree barren; and He pronounced a curse upon it, and went on His way. Mark interleaves the tree and the temple, so that our minds can go from one to the other and back again and leave a question hanging in the air. Will the king come also to the temple and find it barren? And will it therefore also suffer the curse and the destruction which was visited upon the fig tree?

Therefore watch the Lord Jesus. In Mark's Gospel, He tarries in the temple. Beloved, He is seeking fruit! First, He cleanses the temple so as to give it, we might say, a fresh start. He will give people every chance. And in verse 27, they come again to the temple, and He is walking about. It's been cleared of the impediments, He is free to walk around its open spaces, and they begin to come to Him. We've seen it: the ecclesiastical rulers, the Pharisees, the Sadducees, the scribes – and all the time the ordinary folk listening to Him; and they come with their questions thinking they are going to test Him, and He replies with questions by which He sifts them. For the king is coming to a temple which may be showing many fair leaves – but He is looking for fruit.

In 13:1 there is written that disastrous, dramatic word, 'He went forth out of the temple.' He sat until He was sure that there was nothing there that would satisfy His hunger, and He turned His back on the temple, never to enter it again, leaving it with the words, 'Do you see these great buildings? There shall not be left here one stone upon another . . .'

Our question in this study is therefore this: What is it, in His people, that will satisfy the hunger of the king?

**Four interviews with representatives of the people of God**

There are key points in these four interviews, which Jesus had with representative sections of the then people of God.

In 11:27, members of the *Sanhedrin*, the governing body of the Jewish church, come to him and ask, 'By what authority . . .?' Jesus, in a sense refusing their question, replies with a parable. It is told in the opening verses of chapter 12. The vineyard-owner sent servant after servant to his vineyard; after each in turn was rejected, he sent his only son. The Lord answered the question in the revelation of Himself as the only Son of God. The key thought in this interview is sonship. 'By what authority?' they demand. In effect, Jesus answers, 'By my authority as the only Son of God.' And those who would satisfy the hunger of the king, must acknowledge Him as the only Son of God.

The key phrase in the interview with the *Pharisees*, it seems to me, is found in the middle of 12:14: 'You do not regard,' they say to Him, 'the person of men, but in regard for the truth you teach the way of God.' There is a distinctive life-style for the people of God living in all the complexities of this life, with its conflicting loyalties and conflicting claims; and those who would satisfy the king's hunger must follow Him as the way.

The *Sadducees* come, and they would puzzle Him with a hard question concerning eternal life. The Lord Jesus replies authoritatively from the Scriptures. The key verse is verse 24. 'Is it not for this cause that you err, that you know not the Scriptures, nor the power of God?' They come face to face with Jesus who can bring out of the Scriptures the truth which answers questions concerning what truth is. Those who would satisfy the king's hunger must hear the truth from His lips, out of the Word of God.

Finally the *scribes* come. Their question has to do with the interpretation of the law. 'Which is the great commandment in the law? We want to pick our way with subtlety and discernment through all the commandments that God has given, so as to put first things first.' The Lord Jesus sits among them as the authoritative teacher of God's law, and those who would satisfy the hunger of the king must find in Him the life that matches God's requirements.

Now there in one sweep is what, it seems to me, Jesus is teaching His people as He answers their questions. Those who follow the king acknowledge Him as the only Son; follow Him as the way; hear from Him the truth; and find in Him the life. In John's Gospel it is at this point in His teaching that Jesus begins to instruct His disciples about the fact that He is the way, the truth and the life. We need not therefore be surprised that this is the centre of His teaching as He brings His people through this area of contact with Himself and seeks from them the fruit which satisfies the king's heart.

Let us look then at these four incidents again in a little more detail.

### The members of the Sanhedrin come to Jesus (11:27-12:12)

The members of the Sanhedrin ask a very clever question. 'By what authority do you do these things?'

No matter what Jesus says in reply He's going to be wrong, He's going to be accused. If He says 'In My authority as God', they will accuse him of blasphemy. If He says, 'In my authority as man', they will accuse Him of treason, of setting Himself up as a king. And if He says 'Well, I have no special authority', they will accuse Him of being a pretender and an imposter. So they ask a very clever, barbed question. And the answer of the Lord Jesus is equally clever and not at all evasive. He says, 'I will ask you a question,' and He's quite insistent about it. Notice how He says 'Answer me,' twice over (verses 29,30).

This is not evasive, not a debating point; it's serious. He is saying to them: 'Look, if you had followed through the working of God which came to its climax in John the Baptiser, if you knew about the work of God in the prophets – then you would know who I am.' Then in chapter 12 He tells them that lovely story. 'There was a man, who kept sending . . .' In verses 2,4 and 5, 'he sent . . .' Jeremiah tells us (Jeremiah 7:25, Revised Version – some versions miss the exact translation) that God rises up early and sends the prophets. He is keen to send prophets to His people. And if you follow the meaning of that sequence of 'sending', you will appreciate the significance of that final 'sending'. What an amazing history of the mercy of God! Matthew simply tells the fact – there was a final sending. Luke emphasises that it was a deliberate act of God. And Mark underlines the preciousness of the gift. Verse 6: 'He had yet one, a son, a beloved, he sent him.'

The husbandmen planned to kill the son so that 'the inheritance will be ours'. Well, of course, in our legal system nothing of the sort would happen. What lies behind their certainty that they will inherit if they kill the son? They must have assumed that ownerless property was 'up for grabs', and that sitting tenants would be in a privileged position. Now interestingly enough, that was true in the law of the land at that time. They were acting according to the legal forms of which they were aware. But do you see the assumption they are making? They are assuming that the owner is dead. If he is not, the killing of the heir will achieve nothing. Why do they assume that the owner is dead?

Oh, my beloved, listen to me – they must have said to themselves, 'What living father would send his only son to people like us? He must be dead.' Do you see the incredible mercy of God? That He sent His Son last of all?

And in the sending of the son (verse 9) there was a sense of destiny; 'he will come and destroy.' But in the sending of the son there was a revelation of Jesus. Here He is! 'He has yet one, a son.' The Lord Jesus is revealed as the only Son of God!

### The Herodians and the Pharisees come to Jesus (12:13-17)

The question concerning taxes was true to these people's life-style and problems. The Roman poll tax was imposed on subject nations. The Herodians, who were political compromisers, paid it willingly. The Pharisees paid it, but would rather not have to.

The Lord Jesus declares Himself to be the One who can affirm an authoritative life-style for the people of God. He sends for a coin; examines it; asks questions about it. And He says, 'Render unto Caesar the things that are Caesar's, and to God the things that are God's' (verse 17). It is

neither the hesitating 'yes' of the Pharisees nor the
unhesitating 'yes' of the Herodians. Jesus's answer sets up
a new life-style for the people of God, which recognises
God's providence as One who ordains the powers-that-be,
and that recognises God's claims as the One to whom the
due must also be rendered. A life-style of conformity, since
the people of God live in this world and must obey the
lawful demands of the State; a life-style of distinctiveness,
since they also belong to God and must render to Him His
due; and a life-style of comprehensiveness that holds these
two sometimes conflicting factors in a complementary and
whole way. He answers the question in a way that claims
for Him the authority to declare the life-style of the people
of God, so that those who would live under the rule of the
king must seek their life-style from Him and follow Him in
the way.

## The Sadducees come to Jesus (12:18-27)

The Sadducees have a very barbed hook on which to catch
the king. 'This business of eternal life – well, now, you
know that in the Old Testament the law is laid down that if
a man dies childless his brother must take the widow, and
the child born of the union will be reckoned to the
deceased brother and enter into his inheritance. Now then!
There were seven brothers, and the first had her to wife,
and no children, and the second, and no children, and the
third likewise, and the fourth, and the fifth, and the sixth,
and the seventh died, and last of all the woman died . . .
What are you to make of heaven,' they conclude, 'in the
light of that?'

Jesus says, 'It is for this cause that you err, that you do
not know the Scriptures neither the power of God.' What
is His affirmation here? It is that God has spoken, and He
is able to bring to pass what He has declared. Human logic
may declare it inconceivable, laughable or impossible, but
what God has said in His word, He has the power to do.

'You err . . . and the Lord has affirmed an eternal life, with Himself, because He is the God of Abraham, Isaac and Jacob.' And in the Old Testament that does not mean that He is the God whom Abraham chose. It means that He is the God who chose Abraham. It means that in the face of every hazard which life could offer, the true and living God had laid hold on him. And if that is so, He is sufficient to bear him through the final earthly hazard and bestow upon him the final earthly blessing of dying in the hand of God. So our Lord affirms eternal life, and takes His royal place in the midst of His people as the teacher of eternal truth, the One who authenticates the Scriptures as the Word of God.

## The scribe comes to Jesus (12:28-40)

Finally, a scribe came. The scribes were the professional theologians (though they were not in fact allowed to accept payment for their work – it was a sort of free professionalism). They affirmed a piety of human endeavour – 'Get to heaven by works'.

Now if you're going to get to heaven by works you've only a limited time, and you must make the best use of it; so which are the most profitable commandments of the law? 'We haven't time to fiddle around with things that don't bring us much currency in heaven. We want to know what are the leading commandments of the law.' The Lord Jesus replies: 'Such divisions in the law are wrong' (12:29). You cannot pick and choose amongst the commandments, says Jesus: they all come from one God. From the apparently greatest to the apparently least, they are all reflections of the will of the God who is one. The Lord has spoken, and out of His indivisible unity He has declared His indivisible law. So it's not a matter of saying, 'Within my limitation of threescore years and ten I will concentrate on the things which bring me greatest profit, and cut my losses on the things which seem to bring me least profit.'

There is a great principle, says the Lord Jesus, which should infill everything you do; you are to love the Lord your God with all your heart and with all your soul and with all your strength and with all your mind. You are to love Him, and it's got to show in everything you do. Love Him with every inner power, with all your personal commitment, with your whole mental grasp of His truth, and with every personal ability and energy. Just love Him, and let that fill all you do.

'That's the first thing about the law of God,' says Jesus. 'And then, love your neighbour as yourself.'

Do you love yourself? When you wake in the morning and look in a mirror, do you say, 'My word, there's a lovely person; I do love that person!'? We care for ourselves even when we hate ourselves! We are to love our neighbour with a caring compassion, which will fill the whole of life. The Lord Jesus condemned the scribes because they were not loving the Lord their God with all their mind. Verse 35: 'How do the scribes say that the Christ is the son of David, when Scripture says that He is David's Lord? You're not facing up to the reality that the Word of God predicts; a Messiah both human and divine. And you're not loving people with your mind' (verse 38).

Neither towards man nor towards God did the king find that which satisfied His hunger; a true love-filled obedience to the law of God, the life of which God approves.

So there He is; there's the king. And those who would satisfy His hunger see Him as the only Son, follow Him as their way, listen to Him as the truth of God, and obey Him as life, following God's commandments, God-ward and man-ward, in a spirit of love.

### The hunger of the king

We have not yet spoken of the one thing that the king looked for when He came hungry to His city. I want to end with the hunger of the king and the one thing that will meet it. Even more important, you may ask, than seeing Him as the only Son, following Him as the way, listening to Him as the truth and obeying Him as the life? Well, I would not dare to say that, but I will dare to say this: it was the thing that He looked for first.

Come back to Mark 47:10, in the beginning of our passage. The crowd rebuked Bartimaeus: 'Oh, the king can't be bothered with you – don't stop Him; it's all glory, we're on our way to Jerusalem; He's the king coming into His kingdom.' For, as Luke tells us, they thought that the kingdom of heaven was about to appear.

But the king hears prayer. He brings into His presence those who pray. 'Call ye him!' And, says Mark, he cast away his garment and sprang up and came right to where Jesus was; right up (it says in Mark's Greek) to Jesus.

The king unexpectedly teaches about prayer. 'They . . . saw the fig tree withered away' (11:20) – and Peter wanted an explanation. What did Jesus say? Nothing about the fig tree. 'Have faith in God . . .' He turns, from the subject of interest to Peter, to the subject of interest to the king. He teaches about prayer.

The king hungers for a praying people. Verse 15: 'And He taught them, saying, Is it not written, My house shall be a house of prayer?'

When He came among the people of God He lifted up the leaves, He saw all that was legitimately going on in preparing for the authorised worship of God; the changing of foreign currency into Palestinian currency so that sacrifices might be bought for the glory of the God of Israel as He commanded in His word. He saw all that was legitimately going on in the house, and to Him it was all leaves, and He looked under the leaf for the fig. 'My house shall be called a house of prayer.'

The king is hungry, my brothers and sisters, for a praying people. Oh yes, yes! We see Him as the only Son, and, yes, we would long to follow Him in the way and listen to His word as the truth, and obey Him as the life—yes! yes! yes! These are all the marks of those who follow along with the king. But when He came to His people, the first thing He looked for was that His house was a house of prayer—and it was not so! The king's hunger would have been satisfied by a praying people—so may it be satisfied among us here today.

# 2. The Coming Glory of the King's Great Day (Mark 13)

We come into a very privileged place as we come to Mark's Gospel chapter 13, and the very heart of that privilege is expressed in 13:3. For the second time in the Gospel of Mark the Lord Jesus Christ enters into a private place to give private instruction to those who are His very own. There is a very telling phrase used on that other occasion, in Mark 4:34: 'He expounded all things privately to His own.' The lovely rhyming effect in the Greek could be rendered 'on their very own to His very own'. Does that give you the sense of being shut in with our Lord Jesus Christ? Just twice in the Gospel we have that special situation where He puts His own private fence around the Church and says, 'This is something from my mouth for your ears.' On that first occasion He spoke to them in parables, and on this occasion He speaks to them in prophecy.

Our Lord Jesus Christ is a careful Lord, and it must be that He was aware that there is little that frets our spirits and disables us so much as believers more than a sense of aimlessness, a wondering where things are going and what is happening. In order to guard us against that very pernicious enemy of the faith, He twice brings us into a private place and says in effect, 'It's all right, things are working out perfectly well, and the result is going to be glorious.'

## Jesus speaks to the disciples in parables (Mark 4)

The first time, He spoke to them in parables of the triumph of His Word. Mark is very sparing in his Gospel, and He brings us only three parables from that private teaching session: the parable of the sower, the parable of the seed growing secretly, and the parable of the mustard seed. Notice that they are all parables of the seed which is the Word of God, beginning, growing and maturing; the triumph of the Word. The sower illustrates beginnings, the sowing of the seed, how it is resisted and then received; the parable of the seed growing secretly stresses the growth of the Word – the seed grows of its own vitality, the sower knows not how; and the parable of the mustard seed is the parable of the maturing of the Word, when the great tree comes into being and the birds of the air take grateful shelter under its branches. The tree has reached full maturity, and becomes a place of homecoming and of safety.

The Lord Jesus faces us with three situations which are so common in daily life. He faces us with the situation where nothing seems to be going right, and the Word seems to be resisted more often than it is received, and to come to nothing more often than it bears fruit. And He says, 'It's all right; the word will triumph.' Then, He faces us with the situation where nothing seems to have happened because the seed has disappeared into the ground and there is no sign of it. The temptation is to dig it up and see if it is all right, but the Lord Jesus says, 'Oh, though it tarry, wait for it – it's going to be all right, it will grow.' Finally, the parable of the mustard seed comes to us at the moment when we get frightened because everything seems to be changing. A tiny seed was planted and suddenly it's a tree and everything is different, everything is changing, and He says 'Don't worry; it's the maturing process of the Word; and the end will be glorious.'

You see how He speaks to us with reassurance when our hearts would grow fretful under the pressures of the age? And so in our passage today. He takes us privately into His own company. He speaks here not so much of the triumph of His word, but the triumph of Himself, of the sure coming of the king's great day.

## Jesus speaks to the disciples in prophecy (Mark 13)

The people of God were threatened by the structures of the world: the Jewish church and synagogue, the empire and the imperial court with their challenge and opposition to the church. It was a situation of opposition and challenge, of waiting through events of which Jesus says, 'but the end is not yet', a situation where nothing seems to be happening and there is no glimmer of the approaching king. It was a situation for holding on and persevering. 'He that endures to the end shall be saved' – not that his endurance is the road to salvation; but that his endurance is his assurance, that he belongs to the saved.

Endurance, perseverance; but at the end a glory, a gathering together, and an eternal security. It begins with the sowing of the word: Mark 13:10, 'The word must be preached.' When the going is hard it calls for perseverance (13:13), and it ends (13:27) with a homecoming to the king.

You see how the two great teaching sessions belong together? How they fit together and come to us with power, with the identical message of the beginning of the gospel and the perseverance of the saints and the homecoming in the day of maturity and glory. Such is our message from the word of God for today, and what a message of glory and strength it is.

And here we have the king Himself speaking to us. Just look again at verse 3 and savour it. They asked Him privately; He brought them into the secret place with Himself; He said, Come and learn.

## The setting of the discourse

He spoke, as He sat on the Mount of Olives opposite the temple, in a setting of threatened and inevitable judgement (13:1-3). It is as if Mark wrote those first three verses in that way so as to relate them closely to each other; as though he wants us to note particularly where the journey begins and where it ends. It begins as Jesus is on the move through and out of the temple. It ends as He arrives opposite the temple on the Mount of Olives and sits down.

We saw in our previous study how often Mark dips back into the scriptures of the Old Covenant in order to help us to understand those of the New – for the Bible is one covenantal document – and here he reaches back to one of the dramatic high points of the Old Testament in Ezekiel 9, 10, and 11. Ezekiel is given an awe-inspiring vision of the glory of God; and he sees the glory moving. In Ezekiel 9:3 the glory of the God of Israel is on the threshold of the temple, He has left His temple and is standing at the door; in 10:18, the glory of the God of Israel moves from the threshold to the East Gate, God is on His way out of the temple; and in 11:23, the glory of God passes through the East Gate and takes its station on a mountain to the east of the city. 'Do you see what is happening?' says Mark. 'Do you see about whom I am talking, and the significance of this event? The God of Israel is leaving His house, and is taking up the position of one pronouncing an inevitable judgement. The blighting of the fig tree is about to be realised in the blighting of that to which the fig tree pointed – a house and a city and a professing people of God who showed all the leaves of their profession but had no fruit hiding beneath their leaves.

## The disciples' question, and Jesus' answer

The answer that Jesus gives to John and Andrew's

question of verse 4 is wider than the question that was asked: 'Tell us: when shall these things be, and what shall be the sign that these things are all about to be accomplished?' There can be no doubt what the question meant. Jesus had walked with them through the temple, and they had pointed to the magnificence of the buildings and the stonework; and Jesus said, 'The day is coming when it will all be thrown down. And these stones, magnificent and huge as they are, shall not be left even one upon another.'

And so their question concerned 'these things' – the foretold destruction of the Jerusalem temple. Jesus answers it in verse 23 when, picking up the wording of the question, He says, 'Take heed; I have told you all things beforehand.' What is the sign, they asked, that these things are all to be accomplished? He says: Now I have told you all things. Further, they asked him in verse 4: When shall these things be? In verses 29 and 30 He tells them when. So they asked Him about the temple and He predicted concerning it; He answered their question.

But He went beyond that answer. He furnished more than they asked. He alerted them to a process which has a beginning and an end, a first and a last. In verse 7 He speaks of an end; in verse 8, of a beginning. In verse 10 He speaks of a 'first' – 'the gospel must first be preached'; in verse 13 He speaks of a consummation, of the end to which the saved endure.

What is this end, of which Jesus speaks? Is it the destruction of the temple – is that the consummation? No, it is not; the process which has beginning and end is a wider process within which the temple and its affairs are enfolded but which is not exhausted by the history of the Jerusalem temple. There is a distinction made. Verse 23: 'I have answered your question,' says Jesus. 'But . . .'

He looks on and beyond. There is something else, and that something else is 'those days' – the end. In verse 29 again; 'When you see these things coming' – then know that it, the great judgement day, is near, is at the doors. In verse 32 He points the disciples away and beyond, He answers their question but goes on to speak of a first and a last, a beginning and an end. The beginning is the preaching of the gospel; the end is the coming of the king.

So the answer is wider than the question. It speaks of that which alarmed the disciples – 'this temple will be thrown down'. But the Lord Jesus goes on to speak of that which will elate them, and give them the characteristic upward and onward perspective of a believing church, looking for the coming of the Son of Man and our gathering to be with Him.

Let us rejoice together in the possession of the Word that speaks of these things, and in the expectation of the Lord of whom that Word speaks. Let us rejoice together in the elating hope of the coming of our Lord Jesus Christ.


**Jesus begins His discourse (13:5-13)**

So our chapter speaks of the Lord addressing Himself to the point where we will need a confident view of the future, speaking firstly to His own about the dreadful coming events through which they would live, and lifting their gaze upwards to that even greater coming event which would hold them steady in confident expectation.

Let us now look in some detail at Jesus' actual words in reply to the question asked in verse 4. The verses 5 to 13 are a general background introduction. The Lord Jesus does not come to the actual answer to the question until verse 14. He starts by standing back from it, painting in a background, giving it a context. Verse 5 alerts us to this – 'He began to say', or as we might put it, 'He began by saying'.

Presently He will answer the disciples' question, but He wants them to learn something else first. He begins by showing them the state of the world (5-8), and then the experience of the church (9-13). In both these sections, you will see, we have the key expressions about a beginning and an ending. When He speaks of the state of the world He is speaking about something that will be so from the beginning, right to the end. When He speaks of the experience of the church, He is speaking about something that will start with the preaching of the gospel (verse 10), and will go right on (verse 13) to the point where true believers will endure to the end and enter into salvation. It's a background that stretches, you might say, right from the first coming of the Lord Jesus to His second coming.

### The state of the world (13:5-8)
He speaks of the world's religious state, its political state, and its natural state. Its religious state – verse 5: the world will always be preoccupied with false religion and false messiahs. Its political state – verses 7 and 8: the world will always be beset by wars and rumours of wars. And, in the latter part of verse 8, He speaks of the state of nature, the world's natural forces: 'There will be earthquakes . . . and famines . . . and these are the beginning.'

### The experience of the church (13:9-13)
The church experiences opposition from the structures of this world. 'They will deliver you to councils, and you will stand before governors and kings.' By other, antagonistic religious institutions, by the power of the state and its structures, the church will be opposed. Not all the time; not incessantly; but it is a characteristic of the experience of the church between the first coming and the end, that it will find opposition. It will extend (verse 12) to opposition not just from structures but from people, and very intimate people at that, as brother delivers up brother to death, fathers deliver up their children, and children rise up against parents.

The divisive element, which always comes in when there is a true hold on Christ, will take tragic effect. But within this situation are two things equally characteristic of the

church between the 'comings'. In verse 11, there is the
presence and operation of the Spirit of God. There is a
lovely thought here which appears if you compare the
Gospels. In Luke, Jesus says 'I will give you a mouth and
wisdom'; in Matthew, 'the Spirit of your Father'. So the
church is garrisoned by the Holy Trinity, Father, Son and
Holy Spirit. Secondly, the church is called to endurance,
perseverance, persistence (verse 13). Let me repeat,
endurance is not a ladder to salvation; it is the hallmark of
reality on those who are saved, a confirmation to their
spirits that they are in Christ and secure in the day of His
coming.

So the Lord Jesus begins His reply back in time, between
the beginning and the end.


**The heart of Jesus' discourse (13:14-27)**

Now He comes to the meat of His reply; and in verses 14 to
23 He speaks of

*The coming tribulation in Judea*
Now it may be that in these verses we have a little preview
of what other scriptures speak of as times of tribulation,
particularly associated with the return of the Lord Jesus. It
may be that they picked up a clue here, but I want you to
see, apart from what other scriptures may indicate, three
things that Jesus is speaking of here. It is a local tribulation
(verse 14); it is going to happen in Judea. It will be possible
to flee from it ('Flee in that day'). And it will be a
tribulation which will be followed by time, and other
tribulations (verse 19: 'there has not been the like from the
beginning . . . until now . . . and never shall be'); the
implication is that after that particular tribulation time will
go on and there will be other tribulations which will be
comparable but which will not reach the same pitch of
severity.

There is so much in this passage that is mysterious. What

does 'the abomination of desolation' mean? I don't know, and I am not sure that anybody else knows. Part of the excitement of having an inexhaustible Bible is that Scripture is full of mysteries – 'Safe enough for a child to paddle in, yet deep enough for an elephant to swim in', as somebody remarked. Of course there are mysteries. Some say that the 'abomination of desolation' was fulfilled in AD 70 when the Romans set up their legionary standards in the temple at Jerusalem and in the Holy Place. That doesn't make sense to me, because by then it wouldn't be a sign to flee, it would be a sign that it was too late. In Luke He says 'When you see Jerusalem surrounded by armies . . .', and people say that it means the army of Rome camping around the city of God; but what is the point of telling the people to flee if the city is already under siege? The historians do say that allied armies came to the aid of Jerusalem and (quite ineffectually) ringed the city with their forces before the Romans arrived; that may have been the sign that Jesus gave. The reference to the 'abomination of desolation' standing where it ought not to stand may have been in relation to some of the Jewish people themselves; the zealots, defiling the Holy Place by making it the headquarters of their resistance – I don't know.

Jesus is speaking here of something that will be a clear sign to the church then. 'Watch for it,' He says, 'and when you see it, flee,' for it will be the severest trial in the whole course of creation history. And that (verse 23) is the 'all things' about which they asked: 'When will these things happen?'

The second part of Jesus' answer is an answer to the question which Mark does not record but Matthew does: What is it that upholds a believing church through days of great grimness and travail? The answer is,

*The expectation of a coming Lord*
'As you look forward,' says Jesus, 'you will see a mountain

peak of tribulation on its way. Look just beyond it. What do you see? An even greater peak, and it is alight with all the glory of God; for it is the coming of the Son of Man in clouds and glory.'

He speaks to us of an immediacy of expectation. Now He will come – now He will come, and the foolish ones of the earth say – 'Ah, but He didn't come; He was mistaken, and the New Testament scriptures were wrong.' No: the Lord Jesus speaks of that which was then true and is now true and always will be true until He comes again, however long in the providence of God that may be delayed. He Himself has written one word – 'now'. He will come.

The church is waiting to be gathered, and the church will be gathered in those days. That day will be marked by unmistakable, creation-wide foreshadowings; the sun will be darkened, the moon not give her light, the stars fall from heaven. Again, I don't know what that means. Could it be that those who are alive in the great and terrible day of the Lord will have the awesome experience of seeing the universe brought into a new configuration? People will say, 'What is coming?' and the church will answer, 'The Son of Man is coming; are you ready for Him?' Unmistakable events – no hole-in-corner Messiah, nothing in secret, but something that the universe itself rushes to proclaim. A visible and glorious coming! 'And then they shall see the Son of Man.'

Do you notice the word 'they'? The Lord Jesus has been speaking to people who will live through the other tribulation (verse 30: 'this generation shall not pass away'); but when He looks forward to that day, He says 'they'. He knows what He is talking about. It is an immediate coming, the church must live on tip-toe; but He knows that it is not for those to whom He is speaking, this visible and glorious coming together and universal gathering unto Him (verse 27).

## Jesus concludes His discourse (13:28-31)

He enfolds the whole of His great talk to His private ones in a conclusion.

'From the fig tree learn a parable' (how marvellously He reaches back to that from which He began!). Learn from the dread parable of the fig tree which was all leaves and no fruit; it is a portent of judgement to come. 'This will happen' – Jerusalem and its temple will be brought to an end. There is a course of events that can be discerned; the ominous sign of the fig tree, the day of the blighting, is drawing near, it is 'even at the doors' (verse 29). In verse 30 He says 'Watch for it; you, 'this generation' are going to live through it' – He is speaking in direct answer to their question and enforcing His message upon them – 'Learn from what I have said, it is going to happen, you will need my words.' What a lovely, calm certainty there is in verse 31: 'Heaven and earth shall pass away, but my words shall not pass away.'

But alongside that discernible course of events there is a day without a date (verse 32). Be astonished by this: 'Of that day and of that hour no one knows.' The angels don't know. Go higher in the scale of being. 'Neither the Son' knows. Here is something that is mysterious within the Holy Trinity, that is locked away in the counsels of the Father – the day when the Lord Jesus Christ will be manifested in all His glory to a wondering and shocked world and an admiring and rejoicing church. We cannot know the date; so the proper attitude for the believer is one of watchfulness and working, of waiting and praying, of staying alert (13:33-37).

## The people of the coming king

I focus these final thoughts on the people of the coming king, for that is the emphasis of the chapter.

1.  They are *the elect people*. It is a beautiful, glorious,

lovely, gentle word. They are the elect, the chosen beloved ones in whom His soul rejoices. Look at verse 20. Did you know that the whole of world history is run in your interests? The elect are at the centre of the historical workings of God. Verse 22, the elect are in secure possession of the truth, from which they cannot be moved; verse 27, they are possessors of a glorious and certain hope and of a meeting with the coming Lord. They are the elect ones, He chose them because He wanted them.

2. The elect people are *gospel people*, people who know and possess the truth. The world will always try to lead them away from the truth, but they cannot be separated from it. And they are in the world to preach gospel truth (verse 10, 'the gospel must first be preached').

3. Thirdly, they are *praying people*. Look at them in the middle of the severest tribulation that creation will ever know; what are they doing? Verse 18 – they are praying. They are not setting up relief organisations, though that is a good thing to do in itself. They are doing their own distinctive thing, that which no one else can contribute to the history of the world. The elect people are called upon to contribute; not to detach themselves from relief work or from other involvement in the welfare and good of the world in which they are placed, but never to forget that the one ingredient that they can contribute and no one else can is to be a praying company in the midst of world tribulation.

4. They are *an obedient, watchful and committed people*. Look at the end of chapter 12, the story of the widow and her two mites. I said yesterday that nothing in the Word of God is there by accident, everything is selected and deliberate. The Lord Jesus looked around His temple and saw no fruit; but His careful and roving eye lighted upon one who there, in the midst of all the falsity, was a mirror of the truth (12:43).

What a marvellous bridge from the falseness and hollowness and fruitlessness of the temple, to this picture of the fruitful people of God waiting for their coming king! A people modelled on the widow; who hold nothing back; who give, not because their gift has great value, but just for the sake of giving; who rest trustfully for the future upon the one to whom the gift is made; the people of the coming king.

# 3. The Two Feasts and the Two Foes (Mark 14:1-52)

At the beginning of chapter 14 Mark writes, 'After two days was the Feast of the Passover.' But then in verse 3 he speaks of a party that was given for Jesus in Bethany. Now John tells us, in chapter 12 verse 1, that the party happened six days before the Passover. You see what Mark is doing: he's saying 'Yes, it happened earlier, but I put it in now because it's now that you need the message of this feast at Bethany, it's now that you need to see Jesus as He was displayed then.' So having established a careful dating in verse 1 he introduces us to certain background material. Thus once more, by careful selection and combination of the material he has chosen, he begins to build up the portrait of the Lord Jesus which the Holy Spirit, by inspiration, is teaching him.

And how carefully this story is put together! The passage we are considering contains three stories. The story of the party at Bethany and Jesus' anointing by an unnamed woman, verses 3-9; the story of what we foolishly call the Last Supper (it was actually the First Supper, but we have a way of getting things the wrong way round), verses 12-26; and the Gethsemane story, which begins in verse 32. All three are contained in a continuing narrative which Mark allows to flow in and around them;

the story of the plot, betrayal, desertion and arrest. See how he does it.

On each side of the story of the feast at Bethany is a story of secret plotting (verses 1 and 10). When he tells the story of the supper, he does the thing in reverse – he breaks the story up into two parts (12-16, preparing the supper; 22-25, eating it). But at the heart of the story, not bracketing it like the previous one, there is this intrusive element, when Jesus breaks in upon the happiness of the feast with the news that He is aware that He is going to be betrayed (verse 17). And then there's the third story, the story of our Lord in the Garden of Gethsemane, and Mark brackets it round with the story of desertion and arrest (verse 27, predicting the scattering of His followers; and verse 46, the prediction fulfilled as the smiting of the shepherd begins with His arrest). And the narrative ends (verse 50) with 'they all left Him and fled.'

So you see what this is saying to us. Nothing, I repeat, is in the Bible by accident; and so this structure of the fifty verses is meant to teach us how we are at least to begin to understand the three main stories. The primary meaning of each of them, according to Mark, is to be seen in the context of what is put with them.

Two nights are involved in the three stories; the separate night of the party at Bethany, and the single night in which the supper was kept, and Jesus went to the garden, and was arrested. We'll use that night-time scene to provide headings for our study, and talk a little first about the night at Bethany.

## The night in which Jesus was adored (14:1-11)

We will give this a subtitle: 'How worthy He is'. The story is told to reveal what true service is. On the one hand (verse 1) there are the people of status, the chief priests and scribes, the religiously instructed people with all their official status and the opportunity that went with it. On the other hand (verse 10) there is the man of privilege, Judas Iscariot, who – Mark emphasises – 'was one of the twelve'; privileged to be picked out and to walk with Jesus during His ministry and teaching. And in between them, is a woman whom Mark does not name. John tells us the name – it was Mary – but Mark doesn't. He wants to draw attention to the fact that she was unknown.

It was her act that Jesus commended (verse 6); listen to this for a translation – 'She has done a beautiful thing.' She receives, not just a commendation, but a warm delighted commendation, from the Lord. Verse 9: wherever the gospel goes, the record of her deed will go with it.

What did she do? Well, she took a jar of exceedingly precious ointment, worth, we learn, about 300 pence; virtually a year's income, according to the parable of the labourers in the vineyard. She took it, in its beautiful container; the cork was sealed so that it could never be taken out, and all the fragrance of the perfume was there; the only way to release it was to break the jar. She broke that beautiful container and poured all the perfume out upon the Lord Jesus. Upon His head, says Mark. Upon His feet, says John, adding that touch of one who was there, 'the house was filled with the fragrance.' She poured it all out upon Jesus, and Jesus said that it was a beautiful thing.

How worthy He is to receive all, to receive the most precious, to be the first in our devotion and our giving! And how the awfulness of plotting against Jesus and betraying Him is exposed, as an unknown person comes and pours out all. That will go world-wide with the gospel, says Jesus; because that is the response that the gospel and the Lord of the gospel deserve.

I think Mark might have had a second point. This chapter contains two feasts. I think he tells us of one in order to alert us to distinctive features of the second. At Bethany, Jesus is the object of human giving. It's as if

Mark is saying, 'Please note, when you come to the Lord's Supper, it's the other way round' – it is those who are at the table who are the object of all that Jesus has to give. And in verse 9, Mark tells us that Jesus said, 'that which this woman has done will be spoken of for a memorial'; it is remembered by the *telling*, He does not command that it be remembered by re-enacting the breaking of the flask of ointment. But when we come to the Lord's Supper, the supper is to be remembered by the *doing*; the bread is to be broken, the wine shared in the remembrance of our Lord Jesus Christ. So the first feast prepares us by contrast for the second.

**The night in which Jesus was betrayed (14:12-26)**

We give this the subtitle, 'How loving He is'. According to verse 12, Jesus came to what *used* to happen. I think it's a very cunning touch on Mark's part: 'On the first day of unleavened bread, when they used to sacrifice the Passover' (it may not be translated like that in your Bible). When Jesus came to this Passover, it was the last Passover. The feast was about to be superseded and become part of the bygone workings of God.

He came to the last Passover, the first supper, and He focused their attention centrally, obtrusively, upon this: 'One of you shall betray me.' If we are to understand the supper as Mark presents it, we must pay attention to the central feature; a treacherous company. Secondly we must pay attention to the fact that Jesus enfolded the supper in the Passover. You see how deliberately that's done in verses 16, 17 and 22. They were eating the Passover when Jesus made them eat the supper. The supper is enfolded in the Passover. And the third key feature in this narrative of the first supper, the Lord's Supper, is that when Jesus took the Passover bread and wine and used it for this new purpose He used an old explanatory word. Verse 24: 'This is my blood of the covenant.' Three things, therefore, which seem to me to bring out the central understanding of, and provide us with keys to, the Lord's Supper.

First of all, *Jesus deliberately centred the supper on the betrayal* (verse 17). The Passover was a joyous occasion; they were remembering what God had done. Into the joy, He brings a shock: 'One of you shall betray me.' He takes no steps to relieve them of that shock. The murmur goes round, 'Is it I? Surely it is not I?' One of them will, but any of them might; and He leaves them with that thought in their minds. He does not relieve any of them of the treacherous responsibility. He leaves the sense of betrayal brooding over the whole company. It is at the centre of things, obtrusive, shocking. 'One of you shall betray me.' Beloved, as we come to the Lord's Supper, we say this to ourselves as of the first importance: this is a supper for sinners, for those who don't deserve it. How loving He is!

Then secondly, *He wove the supper into the Passover*. He doesn't discard the Passover. They begin to eat it and He brings the supper into it. Neither does He say, Let's celebrate the Passover first and then there's something else I want to do. He doesn't separate the two in that way. So once more we have a key: the supper belongs in the whole scheme of thinking which is the Passover, the sharing of bread and the sharing of wine. It focused, of course, upon the lamb, its death and its flesh; but it was also a sharing of the unleavened bread. As the father of the household, Jesus broke the bread. He may well have used the traditional words: 'This is the bread of affliction which our fathers did eat.' The bread did not become that bread eaten centuries before in Egypt. It was not a miracle but a symbol, full of the power of the reality; an encapsulation of the potent word of God. 'This is the bread of affliction which our fathers did eat' – when we eat it we go back and we become part of that spiritual reality of the people, to whom God came and redeemed them and brought them to Himself. And when the four cups of the Passover feast were passed from hand to hand and shared, they were identified with that four-fold reality: 'I will bring you out, I will rid you of bondage, I will redeem you, I will take you as my people.' They were full of the Passover reality, they brought those participating into that sphere of spiritual reality. And it was that bread and that wine whereof Jesus said, 'Eat this – this is my body; drink this – this is my blood.' He took all that Passover significance and brought it to its finality and completion in the death of the Lamb of God upon Calvary.

Will you turn, please, to Exodus 12; three quick thoughts to focus our minds on what Jesus is doing.

1. The Passover lamb (verse 3) is *a lamb of substitution*. It is a household lamb; it is (verse 4) a lamb equivalent to the number of the people of God; it is a lamb which is equivalent to the needs of the people of God ('. . . according to everyone's eating'). That is the lamb that is going to die. Provision was made, as you know, that if anything of the lamb was left over it should be destroyed unused. It was to safeguard the principle of exact equivalence, so that the lamb that died was the exact equivalent of the people of God: a substitution.

2. Secondly, the lamb is *nourishment*. Verse 12: 'Thus shall you eat it . . .' The lamb is food for pilgrimage.

3. Thirdly, the lamb is *a lamb of propitiation* (verse 13). When God comes in judgement the blood removes the wrath so that He passes over in peace. He has no quarrel with those who shelter beneath the blood of the propitiatory lamb.

And when the people kept the Passover annually they were remembering what God had done once for all, for they came out of Egypt and they can never be brought out again. And the lamb died in their place and can never die again; propitiation has been made so that the former God of wrath is now propitiated towards His people. They go on remembering, remembering, remembering; and Jesus takes the Passover bread and wine, which are caught up with thoughts of substitution, nourishment and propitiation, and He says, 'Look, come and participate in me, my body, my blood.'

4. Finally, *Jesus explained the supper as a covenant sign.* Mark 14:24, 'This is my blood of the covenant.' Covenant signs are some of the most beautiful subjects in the Bible, and ones that in God's goodness are so easy to understand. Think of the rainbow God gave to Noah. Maybe it had never existed before; maybe it always had. At any rate, there it is now in the sky, and God attaches a significance to it. 'When I see the bow, I will remember my covenant.' What God asserts about the sign comes to man with the force of a divine promise. A covenant sign is a proof that the promises are made for you and are operative for you. So when we take the bread and the wine, we say to ourselves – and God by His Spirit says to us – the promises of Calvary are made to us, and those promises operate for us now. 'This is my body.' How loving He is, to come to us with His hands full of Himself!

## The night in which Jesus was enabled (14:27-42)

Now we come to Gethsemane. Are you surprised by our heading? And we have as the central feature of Gethsemane something that will not surprise you at all: 'How prayerful He is'.

According to verses 27-31, the preface to Gethsemane, the Lord Jesus knows that His friends are going to desert Him, and He will be quite alone. According to verse 41, the epilogue to Gethsemane, the Lord is delivered into the hands of His enemies. That is the awfulness of it; not simply the presence of sinners, but the hands of sinners and what those hands will do to Him. So the Lord Jesus comes to the garden with a sensitive anticipation of what lies ahead. As He came into Gethsemane He came into a place of dread (verse 33).

One commentator translates the verbs at the end of verse 34 like this: 'He began to be gripped with a shuddering terror and to be in anguish.' So much was that, so that He testified to His disciples that He believed His hour of death had come. Now the Scriptures don't tell us what lay behind that shuddering terror and gripping anguish. It could have been the extremity of suffering to come; it could have been the loathsome reality of the presence and power of Satan, for Luke tells us in his narrative that the Lord said 'This is your hour and the power of darkness.' It could have been the anticipation of bearing our sin and the revulsion of a totally holy soul from contact with the defilement and contamination of sinners; it could have been the expected alienation from the Father. It could be any of these, or all. But we are told that when He came into Gethsemane He came into a place of dread.

We are told something else. He transformed the place of dread into a place of prayer. In the face of the terror, He fell to praying. How inexpressibly precious are the words at the beginning of verse 35, 'He went forward a little.' Oh, beloved; the Lord Jesus has always gone further forward into the darkness and dread and terror than we will ever go. And He went further forward into the darkness in order that He might enter that darkness as into a place of prayer. And He prayed and He prayed and He prayed again.

Let me share a momentous truth with you. The Lord Jesus came trembling into Gethsemane, gripped with a shuddering terror and an overwhelming anguish of spirit. When He left the garden, according to the record left to us, He never trembled again nor hesitated in the face of the stark realities which had been His terror in the garden. Never again! The place of prayer is the place of power.

That's how He came in; that's how He went out. And this is all He did when He was there. Luke tells us that the anguish went on and on. It was in the second – not the first – period of prayer that the Lord Jesus' sweat became as great drops of blood. So great was His agony; and that was the second period of prayer.

But He came out of His personal agony back to His followers. Why? Not to be strengthened by them, but in order to teach them what He Himself knew; that if they didn't pray, they were sunk. Verse 37: He comes to them and finds them sleeping. 'Stay awake; pray, that you enter not into temptation.' He is determined that they should learn the Gethsemane secret, that the place of prayer is the place of power, that by prayer they will be able to bear the trial which they cannot escape. He says to them in verse 38, 'Watch and pray that you enter not into temptation.' Now, that cannot refer to the experience of trial, for that experience is going to come to them whether they pray or not. Nothing can now stop them coming face to face with their Lord's enemies, and seeing what's going to happen to Him and perhaps, in principle, to them. 'That you enter not into temptation' – that is to say, that it will not take you into its grip and overpower you. The place of power is the place of prayer.

And He adds this word to them in verse 38: 'The spirit indeed is willing, but the flesh is weak.' I want to suggest to you that our Lord, that master of Scripture, is reaching back here to Psalm 51:12. I am so convinced of this that I have replaced the small 's' in this verse in my Bible with a capital 'S'. I have always thought that this verse was saying, 'The Spirit is willing, but the flesh is weak.' You want to, better than you can actually manage. If it were just a matter of 'your spirits' – you'd be at prayer, but your bodies are bringing you down into slumber. And of course that's so often true. But I believe the Lord Jesus is saying something far more significant. The Spirit of God, in all His power, is willing to come to you; but the weakness of your flesh, which is holding you back from prayer, is also holding you back from power.

This matches the experience of our Lord, for we read in Luke's Gospel that when He prayed the more earnestly and His sweat became as great drops of blood – there appeared an angel from heaven strengthening Him. You can have the heavenly strengthening too; you can have the Spirit of God as your power; but only if you enter into the place of prayer. Prayerlessness decides the issue. So when Jesus came back the third time and found them still sleeping, He said that dread word in verse 41: 'It is enough.' It is as if He said, 'That settles it; you and I are now going different ways; you wouldn't come into the place of prayer, therefore you cannot come into the place of power.' The night in which He was enabled and strengthened; because He was prayerful.

## The night in which Jesus was arrested (14:43-52)

We offer as a subtitle here, 'How willing He is.' In the Gethsemane passages the Lord Jesus twice refers to this night as 'the hour'. The high moment of destiny. If you look up references to 'the hour', especially in John's Gospel, you'll find that's true. In Gethsemane, He knows that the hour has come. He prayed first of all (verses 35,36) that 'the hour might pass away'. As He continued in prayer (verse 36) He changed the expression from 'the hour' to 'the cup'. The high moment of destiny is the cup, the climax of His Father's will for Him; the cup which the Father has given Him to drink, which is going to be the cup of the outpoured wrath of God. The cross is the climax of the Father's will.

The passage we've been working through has prepared us for that understanding of the cross. Verse 21: 'The Son of Man goes even as it has been written of Him.' The Father's will has been declared in the Scriptures, and now the hour has come and the cup of wrath must be drained. At the end of the Gethsemane passage Jesus speaks of the hour again: 'The hour has come.' The high moment of destiny has arrived, when sin reaches its peak, in the deliberate rejection, condemnation and execution of the Son of God. And surely the passage has prepared us for that as well. Secret treacherous plotting, treachery and guile at the heart of the apostolic band – 'All of you shall desert me.' Sin is going step by step to its climax, and when the high moment of destiny comes, there will be the hands of sinners.

And in between those two, the drinking of the cup of wrath and the enduring of the malice of man, between the wrath of God against sin and the actual sin against which that wrath is poured, there is the sole figure of our Lord Jesus. No one with Him; all forsake Him. The sole figure of the Lamb of Calvary.

And what is going through His mind at that point? In verse 21, He says 'The Son of Man *is going*.' In verse 41, He says, 'The hour is come, the Son of Man is betrayed; up, *let us be going*.' He is neither the victim of a divinely imposed fate, nor is He a victim of an overwhelming power of man. The cross, which is to be explained as the act of the wrath of God and the act of the sin of man, is also the act of the voluntary Saviour. How willing He is!

There is the very heart of the substitutionary enterprise. If you asked an animal brought to the altar of God, a spotless body which could stand in for my sin-stained body, 'Why are you here?', you would receive no reply. For the animal, which in its spotlessness could well stand in for me in my stain of sin, could not represent me where I was centrally a sinner, in that I had consented to do wrong.

The Lord Jesus comes on the scene and He takes the words of Scripture. He says, 'A body you have prepared for me.' He can bring all the perfection of His human nature, the moral glories of the Christ, to the cross of Calvary. He can bring a spotless body to stand in for my stained and defiled person. But He looks up to the Father and He says: 'Lo, I come to do your will, O my God. I am content to do it.'

All that God had ever longed for, and depicted, and worked for, came to its climax and completion in the voluntary offering of the spotless Son of God. Bearing the divine wrath, bearing the sin of man – content to do it: one sacrifice for sins for ever.

# 4. The Son of God with Power
# (Mark 14:53-16:8)

Our rather long passage falls into three clear divisions. In the first (14:53-15:19) we read how the Lord Jesus came to His death. Step by step He was taken; He was 'led away', 'carried away', 'led out'; and so the Son of God came to the cross. In the second (15:20-16:1) we read what the Lord Jesus accomplished by His death. The passage is full of the reality of the death of the Lord Jesus Christ. It was no pretence; it was a real death, and this is one of the main emphases in this section of Mark's Gospel. In verse 24 he describes the mode of death, crucifixion; in verses 30 and 32, the instrument, the cross. In verse 37 he describes the experience of death. And in verse 43 we are made aware of the finality of it. All that was left for human eye, human hand and human care was a body (verses 44,45). In verse 46 we see that the reality of His death came to its appointed end; that seemed to be the end of it, for when the women came on the Sunday morning, they came to attend the dead. Verse 16:1, 'Mary Magdalene, Mary the mother of Jesus and Salome brought spices that they might come to anoint Him.'

But as He dies on the cross and finally breathes out His last, the Lord Jesus is surrounded in His dying by voices and events. There are three cries of mockery, in verses 29,

31 and 32; then in a rather dramatic way the scene changes and the external voices are hushed, and from verse 33 onwards we have three further circumstances attending the cross. There is firstly (verse 33) the darkness; then the Lord's own cry: 'My God, why hast thou forsaken me?'; and finally, most dramatic of all, the veil of the temple was rent in twain, from the top to the bottom (verse 38). As we study these six items a little later we will find that they declare what Jesus was doing as He died upon the cross. So we can well call this section, 'What the Lord Jesus Christ accomplished by His death'.

The third division, 'How the Lord Jesus triumphed over death', is found in chapter 16 verses 2 to 8.

I end our study of Mark at verse 8 because – as far as our knowledge goes – that is the last point at which we can be certain of having what Mark wrote. There seems to be no doubt (and the fact is recorded in all English translations of the Bible, from the Revised Version of 1881 onwards) that verses 9 to 20 were added at a later date. Mark may have written an ending to his Gospel, but if so, by the will of the Holy Spirit, that ending has been set aside. Just as it was not the mind of the Holy Spirit for us to have Paul's letter to the Laodiceans, so if Mark went on after what we call verse 8 the Holy Spirit has said 'No; the church must not have that.' So we come in verses 1 to 8 to the last that we are certain that we have from Mark's pen. And there in the centre of it is the great angelic testimony of verse 5: 'They entered the tomb and saw a young man sitting on the right side, clothes in a white robe; and they were amazed.' What a lovely contrast that makes with the other young man Mark found clothed with linen, the young man we meet at the beginning of our passage (14:51). Oh, how marvellously that picks up what was then true, that the Lord Jesus was deserted by all, even the carnal onlooker whose name Mark does not record. The Son of God was left alone, and all who would be with Him fled naked and in disarray. The loneliness and desolation of the Son of God, in the hands of His enemies!

Mark takes up the same word to describe the angel who comes bearing great news; that Jesus, whom a terrified young man left in the hands of His enemies, is risen from the dead; and His company now is glorious, clothed in shining garments. 'You seek Jesus of Nazareth,' he says. 'You seek the one who has been crucified. He is risen; He is not here. Come, see the place where He lay, and go and tell.'

That then is how our passage divides; it is long, but it comes to us in well-defined sections, each bringing to us a well-defined area of truth. As we come back to these three sections again for a little more detailed consideration we'll give them different headings.

## The power of His life (14:51-15:20)

We're going to consider the power of His life. And right at the centre of that we're going to consider the theme: the Just in the place of the Unjust. The power of the Lord Jesus Christ's life, and the purpose for which He exercised it.

In this passage Jesus is brought before two courts. He stands first (14:53) before the church court of His day. Then He comes before the state court (15:1). The Lord Jesus was brought before the church court and the state court, the Jewish court and the Gentile court; the whole world in principal arraigns Jesus on trial and condemns Him. Before both courts He manifested His power in the same way.

It was the power to keep silent. Verse 60: 'He held His peace and answered nothing.' It was the power to affirm the truth. Verse 61 'Jesus said, I am. And you shall see the Son of Man sitting at the right hand of power and coming with the clouds of heaven.' What a glorious, firm and – if we can use the word, and I think we can use it more of Jesus than of anybody else – manly, declaration of the truth!

And (verse 65) it was the power to suffer. 'Some began to spit on Him and to cover His face and to buffet Him; and the officers received Him with blows of their hands.'

It was exactly the same when He came to the state court presided over by Pontius Pilate. Chapter 16, verse 2, Pilate asked, 'Are you the king of the Jews?' He answered, 'You say it' – the power to affirm the truth. In verse 4 Pilate asks 'Do you answer nothing? Behold, how many things they keep accusing you of.' But 'Jesus no more answered anything; insomuch that Pilate marvelled' – the power to keep silent. And (verse 15) it was the power to endure suffering. You must have noticed how reticent the Bible is about the actual sufferings of Jesus, and it's not for us to embroider where the Bible only states. He had the power to suffer.

In the church court He suffered at the hands of falsehood. These were men who prided themselves that they were the only people in the world who possessed divine truth. At their hands Jesus suffered falsehood, and made no reply, and accepted what they wished to do to Him. Verse 55: 'The chief priests and the whole council kept seeking witness against Jesus and were not finding it, for many kept bearing false witness.' The people of the truth used the weapons of falsehood. Before Pilate's court Jesus stood before people who prided themselves on giving the world Roman law; and at the hands of Roman law He suffered illegality and accepted it in silence. In each court they proved that at the point where they prided themselves their pride was hollow, and they condemned the Son of God.

Likewise, in each court He suffered gratuitous cruelty. In the court of the high priest they spat on Him and covered His face, inviting Him to prophesy; and the menial court officials received Him from one to the other with b l o w s .

He suffered there a mindless stupidity; they covered His face and invited Him to prophesy because of their absurd misunderstanding of Scripture. In Isaiah 11, it says that when the messianic king comes He will not judge by the seeing of His eyes. By what will He judge, then? asked the Jewish pundits. If He cannot judge by eye He must judge by smell. So they covered His face to test if He was the Messiah or not. The stupidity of those who possessed, but would not listen to, the truth! And in the state court, having been condemned with total illegality, He was subjected to that refinement of torture, scourging; to mockery, the crown of thorns; to torture, which is the final breakdown of every legal system of man.

And the power of the Lord Jesus was the power to endure to the end.

Dear old Peter, who, tradition tells us, is the authority behind Mark's Gospel, never says anything to his own credit in the Gospel, but never conceals anything that is to his detriment. In his honesty he made Mark write down the full story of his betrayal of Jesus without extenuation.

Yet Peter did marvellously well, didn't he? He did begin to follow the Lord again, though he followed Him afar off. He did go right into the house of the high priest even though he was the only one of the disciples against whom a separate charge could be levelled – the slicing off of the ear of the high priest's servant. Yet he went into the place where he could be recognised and charged. Oh, he did well. But at the crunch moment, he didn't do well enough. And yet the Lord Jesus, under infinitely greater provocation, suffering and threat, carried right through to the end with an endurance that knew no limitations. Wherein lies the difference between them? Jesus prayed in Gethsemane; and Peter slept. Jesus said, 'If you do not pray, you cannot but enter into temptation.'

And the power of Jesus was the power to obey. He was led as a sheep to the slaughter, but for His part, the prophet says, 'He humbled Himself and opened not His mouth.' But even more than that, the prophet says, 'He was numbered among the transgressors.'

The choice is placed before the leaders and the people: 'Do you want Jesus? Do you want Barabbas?' I have discovered that nine separate times in the Gospels the innocence and guiltlessness of Jesus is affirmed. Nine times! 'Do you want this man who is nine times over the innocent one? Or do you want this man, the proven insurrectionist, murderer and robber? Which will you have?' And they chose Barabbas, and Jesus carried the cross that Barabbas should have carried. The guilty went free and the innocent died instead.

So Mark's account of Jesus' road to the cross climaxes at this point. Jesus led His obedience to this climactic point; that He was content to be numbered with the transgressors, and to die, the just in the place of the unjust.

The Lord's power to endure carries on, right through the experience of the cross, and we bridge over now to the second section of our study.

## The power of His death (15:21-47)

This time we will use the subtitle 'So great salvation'.

John tells us in his Gospel, in a very striking phrase, (19:17) that Jesus 'went forth bearing the cross for Himself.' Well, how John rejoiced in the vigour of the manhood of Jesus! Notwithstanding the scourging, the mockery, and the crown of thorns, He went forth bearing the cross for Himself. When Mark therefore tells us of Simon of Cyrene in 15:21, he is not telling us of something that was necessary to Jesus. He needed none to carry the cross; He went out carrying it Himself, in the strong manhood of the Son of God. Simon represents a totally unnecessary piece of Roman aggravation, to show their dominance over a subject people.

And He continued in vigour, from the moment He went

forth bearing the cross to the moment recorded in Mark 15:37. Oh, the vigour of that final shout from the cross! He did not die from the usual effects of crucifixion – starvation, exhaustion, suffocation; the Son of God died because He had completed the work that the Father gave Him to do, and He laid down His life of Himself. And what did He achieve thereby? What is the power of accomplishment that is resident in the death of Jesus?

We've seen already that the cross is surrounded by six things; three cries of mockery and three other events which seem to have occurred in dead silence.

Mark selects, out of all that happened, three cries of mockery, because in mockery of what they saw as a failure, these people were really, though quite ignorantly, proclaiming what Jesus was doing and what He had accomplished. The taunt expressed the truth.

First of all, He achieved the true temple. 'Ha!' the cry of mockery went up (verse 29), 'Thou that destroyest the temple!' What the Lord Jesus had said about the temple had rankled in people's minds. This is what He said (John 2:19): 'Destroy this temple, and in three days I will raise it up.' And they were 'astonished and affronted'. It took forty-six years to build, they said; and will you do it in three days? But John adds his careful comment: 'He spake of the temple of His body.'

What is the temple? It is a place where God lives, where He welcomes His accepted people into His presence and keeps them secure by the blood of sacrifice. The Lord Jesus upon the cross, not in a temple of bricks and mortar but in a temple of His own precious body, was creating the true temple of God. Here is where God resides, where He is to be found and approached; in His Son, our Lord Jesus Christ. Here is the shrine into which the redeemed come, through the precious blood, and where they are ever secure in the presence of God. He has accomplished the true temple, for as the Scripture says: 'We were quickened together with Christ, and raised up with Him, and made to sit with Him in earthly places, in Christ Jesus' (Eph. 2:5) – the true temple, the true gathering of the people of God, the true sanctuary of His body and the true precious blood which is our security.

Secondly (verse 31) they cried out about salvation: 'He saved others, He cannot save Himself.' How truly they remembered that Jesus said He had come to seek and save that which was lost. They take up His true claim and make it a taunt and a mockery. 'You can't even save yourself' – how truly they spoke! If others are to be saved then He cannot be saved. There is a necessity about it. If salvation is to be accomplished there is no other way; He must die, He must endure the cross, He must retain the fastenings of the nails. 'One died for all,' says the Scripture. 'Therefore all died.' There is such correspondence between the death which He died and the death which I ought to have died, that when He died, I died. The full penalty with which I was obligated before the throne of heaven was discharged. There is that blessed reality of substitutionary salvation. He is so fully and effectually identified with those for whom He died, that when He died, they died. Their whole penalty and pain was discharged, and the Son of God died in their place.

Thirdly, He achieved the kingdom of Israel. Verse 32: 'Let the Christ, the king of Israel, come down.' Pilate had mocked and scourged Him as the 'king of the Jews' (verse 26); and these people around the cross are going right back to the reality of the thing, they are claiming the name Israel. How blessedly He is the king of Israel, for out of the work of our Lord Jesus Christ there sprang there and then the kingdom of David, His father, and the kingdom of God, His Father. And for all eternity there was established the people of the Israel of God; the fullness of covenantal reality.

What an accomplishment upon the cross! The temple, substitutionary salvation, the people of God – and that's not the end. For when silence came and darkness, and the voices were hushed, a great cry of loneliness arose on Calvary; and nearby, the veil of the temple was rent in twain. All these other accomplishments were summed up in the work of our Lord Jesus on the cross whereby there was a final settlement for sin (verse 33). The whole of the second half of the drama of salvation was shrouded in darkness.

What does your memory say about darkness? It was the last of the plagues of Egypt, wasn't it – the moment of climax of sinful rebellion and resistance to the word of God. As darkness reigned, Pharaoh broke off diplomatic relationships and discussions with Moses. He severed the conversations. He said: 'Go, see my face no more.' It was the end of probation, and the finalisation of sin over the world. Shrouded in that darkness were the whole people of the Gentiles, represented by the Egyptians, and the whole people of God, represented by the Israelites. Nothing now remained but a dreadful expectation of judgement – and so it happened, did it not, in the land of Egypt. Beloved, the Word of God is one book, and it says the same thing throughout. The darkness was followed by the judgement of God upon the firstborn of Egypt.

But into that darkness there came in Egypt and Calvary the Lamb of God. And out of the darkness there came that one and only cry from the cross, which Mark wants us to know about. Others will tell us other things; of whispers from the cross and words from the cross; but here is a great shout from the cross!

In the strong voice of the crucified Lamb of God: 'My God, My God, why have you forsaken me?' This is the strength of His anguish as the pit opens before Him, as He knows in Himself the full reality and weight of the sinner's plight and the sinner's judgement, as He receives upon His holy body the full outpouring of the sinner's penalty: 'My God, why have you forsaken me?' The Scripture says: 'I have never seen the righteous forsaken.' He, the righteous

one, endured that forsaking, when God made Him who knew
no sin, to become sin, on our behalf.

The darkness, the death of the Lamb, and then the end of
the curse; verse 38, 'The veil of the temple was rent in twain,
from the top to the bottom.' Josephus said that it was woven
to the thickness of one inch. It was more like a luxurious
carpet, hanging down, all sixty feet of it, from the ceiling to
the floor. The veil of the temple was rent! The last and greatest
barrier, the inevitable consummation of the inevitable barriers
between a holy God and a race of sinners. And it's gone!

You remember there were three veils in the temple. There
was the veil that hung on the gate of the court, the veil that
hung at the entrance to the tent, and the veil that hung over the
Holy of Holies. Then, as now, there was a way back to God,
and it was marked by three gates. They were all the same; the
curtains were of blue and purple and scarlet and fine twined
linen.

As we look back at them through the magnifying glass of our
Lord Jesus, the Lamb and the Son of God, we see that the blue
is His heavenly origin and divine nature; the purple is His kingly
status and glory; and the scarlet is the blood of His cross. And
the fine twined linen is the moral glory of a perfect humanity.
When all that is rent on the cross, then we can enter in through
the veil – that is to say, His flesh, into the holiest of all.

So that finally, the cross reveals the Lord Jesus. The
centurion stood by the cross. There he is in verse 39; and as
he watched and waited, so also he listened, and he was near
enough to hear. He heard that great cry of verse 37: 'It is
finished.' He heard, too, the whispered prayer with which
our Lord Jesus breathed His last. 'Father, into thy hands I
commend my spirit.' And the centurion heard and
believed. 'Of a truth, this man was the Son of God!'

## The power of His resurrection (16:1-8)

We're going to give this section a subtitle from the middle
of Mark's account: 'He is not here.'

Come straight away to the statement which lies at the heart of Mark's story (verses 6 and 7). The resurrection is not a deceit. The same Jesus died, and rose again. 'You seek Jesus the Nazarene; He is risen.' No deceit. The same Jesus. The resurrection is not a mistake; it's the same tomb — 'Behold, the place where they laid Him.' The tomb is really empty.

The resurrection is a revelation!

As for the fact, they see the empty tomb. But the revelation of God says that the explanation of that empty tomb is that He is risen. That's why, 'He is not here.'

The resurrection is also a seal from God, for Mark's Greek says: 'He has been raised.' Of course He is risen; but behind that, there is an act of somebody else. He has been raised. The resurrection is something that has been done to Him by someone else. Yes, it's the Father, so glorying and delighting and approving in what Jesus did upon the cross, that He says 'I will let the world know what I think about this. I'll raise Him from the dead!'

The tomb was opened, and the stone was rolled away, not to let Jesus out, but to let us in; so that we might know that the Father sealed and approved the work of Calvary. The resurrection is a seal. It is a commission — 'Go and tell.' It is a promise of fellowship — 'Go to Galilee, you will see Him there.' And it is an endorsement of the words and the person of our Lord Jesus Christ. It is all as He said.

In and through all that, there is the one central theme which is the focal point of Mark's testimony to the risen Lord. Each Gospel has its destinctive testimony, and Mark brings his testimony to the risen Lord to one central focal point and issue. Look; the women were there all the time (15:40). They were there, and they saw Him die (15:47). They were there, and they saw Him being buried (16:1).

They had expectations in accordance with what they had seen. They had seen a death, a burial, a body. They said, 'Let us perform the last possible act of love, however gruesome it's going to be. Let us go and anoint the body.'

And those expectations and explanations were in accordance with the facts; they were right. 'Pilate marvelled if He were dead' (15:43). 'And calling to him the centurion, he asked him whether He had died some while ago. And when he heard it of the centurion, he granted the corpse.' He demanded, in other words, a death certificate from the specialists, and got it. So what the women saw was true. All that amounts to the irreversible reality and finality of death.

'And they came to an empty tomb' – and with trembling and astonishment, they heard of a risen Jesus. That is what Mark wants us to know. 'Jesus the Nazarene' – this is the Lord Jesus in the full reality of His human nature. 'Jesus, the crucified' – the one who endured the torment and the mutilation of the cross. 'Jesus, the entombed' – left and sealed in the darkness, because death has had its way with Him; that Jesus. Jesus in the full reality of His person, in the full experience of His sufferings, in the full finality and meaning of his death – that Jesus is risen!

That is what Mark wants us to know.

The power of His resurrection.

The Son of God, with power, through the resurrection from the dead.

# STUDIES IN GENESIS 1-11

*by Rev Philip Hacking*

## 1. Man in God's World
## (Genesis 1 and 2)

Apparently nobody has ever expounded Genesis chapters 1
to 11 from the Keswick platform. Why then am I doing so
today? Well, because I believe that the first eleven chapters
are desperately important for our world. They are not just
the story of how things began; they are the story of the world
in which we live. I do not believe that we can be responsible
Christians without understanding these chapters.

Let me say quite simply, I do not claim to be in any sense
an Old Testament scholar. I am indebted to a superb book
on Genesis. If you buy Derek Kidner's commentary, you
will discover that I read it before you. You will find many
excellent things in it.

Now of course the dangers of studying these chapters are
that some (I hope not many) will come not so much
wanting to hear what God has to say, but to hear what
Philip Hacking has to say on certain controversial issues.
Please may we, before we go any further, ask God to help
us to see the wood and not just the trees? These are great
chapters; I shall not duck the controversial bits, I shall seek
to explain what I believe God to be saying.

In chapter 12 of Genesis, where our studies end, the story
of the church begins; Abraham sets out in faith. I think it

significant that before God unfolds the story of Abraham, He gives us the background of that world out of which the church is called and back into which it will be sent.

Genesis 1-11 is timeless. It has a lot to do with tomorrow's world. Jesus used the story of Noah as a prototype of the final judgement; the story of the tower of Babel with which our study ends is the beginning of the story of Babylon, which ends in Revelation with the fall of 'Babylon the Great'. You will find intriguing little cross-references. Do you realise that the serpent, who is Satan, remains fossilised – at least as a serpent – until Revelation, when it all comes full circle? And there also Eden gets restored, though with some tremendous differences, as we shall see.

So there is much about tomorrow's world, and, yes, there is much about yesterday's world. Of course there is a lot here about how it all began; but please note that the Bible is not so much concerned with how, as why. The big problem is not 'How did it start?' but 'Who is in charge, where is it going, is there any purpose in life?' I find many people are obsessed by the meaninglessness of life; you cannot believe that if you believe Genesis. It tells us why.

There are certain question marks that remain. You will be relieved to hear that I am not a scientist; I resisted the temptation to delve into all the latest theories of evolution and Christian views thereon; I got my nose firmly embedded in Scripture and was not distracted. But what I do know is that it is only false science and superficial theology that clash; a real scientist and a real theologian will find much beautiful harmony in the first chapters of Genesis.

Can I ask you to bear a text in mind? It is one that I believe should be written in letters of gold in every Bible. Deuteronomy 29:29 – 'The secret things belong to the Lord our God' – leave them there! – 'but the things which are revealed belong to us and to our children . . . that we may do them.' And I shall have failed in these Bible readings if we are just excited and intrigued, thrilled and exasperated; but I shall be delighted if we go out to obey. It's very easy to love debating secret things, because we know that there is no final answer. But the things that God reveals to us at Keswick afresh are 'that we might do them'.

So about yesterday's world there will be certain question marks. But that is not all there is in Genesis 1-11: primarily it is about today's world, which is my theme. It was for Moses, using the sources he used (wherever they came from) a revelation of the world in which he lived and had to minister; a revelation of why man was rebellious and sinful and wasted God's world. It is still a picture of God's world; and I defy anybody to understand what is happening in the world outside without knowing and accepting the truth of Genesis 1-11. At the end of 1:31 comes the phrase 'everything He had made . . . was very good.' And then, in 6:5, the very opposite: 'the thoughts of men's hearts were only evil continually.' What has happened in between? Man has fallen. These are still twin pictures today of God's world. The world outside is still 'very good'; and man's heart is 'only evil', apart from the grace of God.

In this Bible Reading we are going to look at two great affirmations. First: this is God's world. Second: this is man's world.

## This is God's world

It is not hard on a lovely day like this at Keswick to believe that this is God's world; but I hope that if you were in the most populated city in the world, on a desperately cold and miserable day, you would still say that this is His world. We must be careful; it is not just the beauty of individual parts of creation – it is the whole that is God's world.

*A creative power*

Would you notice, please, that in verses 1-5 of chapter 1 there are pictures of a creative power? Here is the Trinity. Do you have Jehovah's Witnesses who knock on your door and tell you, within a breath or two, that you cannot find the Trinity anywhere in Scripture? I love them when they get on to that line, because I have to tell them that I cannot get away from the Trinity anywhere in Scripture, page after page; and here He is, right at the beginning, just as He was at the beginning of the life of Jesus. It is a message of the sovereign God. 'In the beginning God created . . .'

The first sentence of Scripture, and .he subject is God. Please, never say the first four words without the fifth. Sometimes people say it is 'In the beginning God . . .', but it is not; it is 'In the beginning God created . . .' – that is, we can only know God because of what He has done. Paul writes (Romans 1:19-21) that even pagans who have not got the law of God 'might know His eternal power and deity through what has been made.' He is the sovereign God, He is at work and we may know Him; He is not an unknown God. It is very interesting that, I believe, in 35 verses from 1:1 to 2:4, God is mentioned 35 times. I know you cannot prove things by statistics, but isn't it a reminder that He is in charge, that He is the sovereign Lord?

The word 'created' comes three times: in verses 1, 21 and 27 – the whole universe, the animal world, and man. God created. 'Out of nothing,' says the Epistle to the Hebrews; a sovereign God. This is the magnificent truth about our God; He made us, in a sense, out of nothing; the world was created out of things which do not appear. A sovereign God.

Secondly, the Spirit of God. Verse 2: chaos and emptiness became form and fullness as the Spirit of God moved over the face of the waters. In the Revised Standard Version the verb is 'moving', and the sense has to do with a bird fluttering, hovering. It is a picture of a bird watching over the waters. I like this; it is the dove that came upon Jesus at His baptism. It is a reminder that God who is sovereign is not distant and far away, He is not way back in time, distant in space, alone; He is here – what the experts call the transcendence and the immanence – He is away but He is here. And the Spirit of God was like a mother bird.

Let me ask you to think this one through. If God is our Father, there is a sense in which the Bible says He is also our Mother. All the qualities of motherhood are there in God – He is both Father and Mother; and the Spirit of God, like a mother bird, is hovering over the face of the waters. To do what? Two things: to bring life, and to bring order. Please note that this is what the Spirit does. He brings life and order, not division and chaos. There He was, and He brought order. Psalm 33:6 – 'By the Word of the Lord the heavens were made, and all their host by the breath of His mouth.' The sovereign God; the Spirit of God.

And the third power in this creative power is the Word of God. Eight times we read 'And God said . . .'

Here is why Genesis is important. You cannot understand the New Testament without understanding the Old Testament; and if you want to understand what God is doing in the New Testament, you need these chapters. We know, as Christians, that Jesus is the Word of God; we know that John 1, like Genesis 1, gives us this picture: 'In the beginning was the Word, and the Word was with God.' In Colossians, Paul reminds us that 'in Christ all things were made.' Pause a second and think; if that baby in the womb of the Virgin Mary was the creator God – how marvellous, how wonderful is love! And if the man strung up on the cross at Calvary was the one whose hands created this world in which we live – how unbelievable! ''Tis mystery all! The Immortal dies!'

Well, there is the Word of God. 'And God said . . .' Have you noticed, that when God said 'Let there be light', there was light? God is involved in light – 'In Him was light and the light was the life of men.' But can I point out to you, that there are myths about creation in other religions which see a kind of conflict between light and darkness, a continuing battle. The Bible does not say that. There is no conflict. God is in charge, and He also made the darkness. I hope you are not afraid of the dark; some adult people are; and I hope that you are not frightened of the dark of the future. The Psalmist learned that 'darkness and light are both alike to you.' So God is the God of the darkness as well as of the light. A creative power.

And will you take with you the thought which I have not time to expound; that all this can be interpreted of the New Creation? 2 Corinthians 4:6 – 'God has shined in our hearts to give us the knowledge of the glory of God in the face of Jesus.'

*A creative pattern*

Now secondly, a creative pattern; and here I notice three works going on. First, what I call *a continuing work*; and here, I suppose, we come to our first controversy.

The symmetry and balance of Genesis 1 is the picture of the days. Now there are those who would want to interpret these as days of revelation to Moses; that he got a revelation of one day, then another day, and then another. Some very distinguished people believe that, and I believe it is something you may accept; although remember the secret things belong to the Lord our God. There are those who believe in terms of a creation in seven twenty-four hour days. I think they are few. And there are many of us who believe that this pictures the kind of balance of creation, the symmetry, the movement; I believe that a 'day' is not a twenty-four hour day. If you look at 2:4, it talks about the whole seven days as being one day – 'In the day that the Lord God made the earth and the heavens'. And with the Lord, a thousand years was one day and one day was a thousand years.

But what it tells us – and this is so important – is that there was a continuing work; a work that moved on to its completion, and day after day it was 'very good'. Let me just throw in another controversial point and then move on. Let's get out of the way that awful word which raises people's hackles: evolution. There are some people in whom it arouses very strange reactions! Let me explain what I think you can be sure of in Scripture. You can be sure, in Scripture, that God is in control and that man is unique. Man is not just the last in the line, the most sophisticated animal. Without these two you do not believe Scripture; and an evolution that says it's just a mechanical process and man is no more than an animal is wrong. That I would state categorically, and no scientist will ever shift me an inch. But having said that, if you look at our verses – for example verses 11 and 12 – it talks about things developing according to their kinds on earth; verses 24 and 25 talk about being fruitful and multiplying; God said, 'Let the earth bring forth living creatures' – He is in charge. Verse 22 – 'Be fruitful and multiply and fill the waters in the seas, and let the birds multiply on the earth.' There is some development and God is in control.

Now there are two lovely things I will just point out in passing (because we can't look at every verse in eleven chapters of Genesis); one of them is at the end of verse 18: 'He made the stars also.' It's a sort of throw-away line. I watch Patrick Moore's television programmes about astronomy, and I am so fascinated by this universe – the galaxies, and stars I cannot even begin to imagine; and all the Bible says is 'He made the stars also.' Just an offshoot of that particular day. Is that not lovely? (If you want a bit more, look up Isaiah 40:26 – 'He knows them all by name' – that is something! – 'and not one of them is missing.') He is in charge.

Every now and then I am asked that great question: Supposing there is life in another galaxy . . .? It does not bother me one iota, but if there is life in some other galaxy

then the God who made it has His plan of salvation for
them as well. The Bible is for those who live here! Don't be
obsessed by what happens there.

One more thing about the stars which needs to be said.
Verse 14 says that they are for signs, and for seasons, and
for days and years. This has got nothing to do with
astrology, the Zodiac or horoscopes. I am appalled that
there are Christians who actually believe all that nonsense.
The stars and fate have no influence on your life. God
made the stars; and it is a continuing work.

Secondly, *a climactic work*. The greatest part of God's
creation is man. Yes, we shall go on in our next study to
realise what man has done with God's world, but man is
the greatest part of God's creation. Not just physically –
we are marvellously made, but over and above that we are
told in verses 26 and 27 that man is made 'in the image of
God'. God had a special debate. 'Let's make man in our
image' – made, says the psalmist, 'a little less than divine'.

Let me say two things about this climactic work. Do you
know that line of awful poetry – I forget who wrote
it – 'One is nearer God's heart in a garden, than anywhere
else on earth'? I don't think that it is true. I am a lot nearer
God's heart with you than I would be in any garden,
because man is made in the image of God, unlike the
animal world, unlike anything else in the universe as far as
we know. And we can say 'No'. We can respond in
disobedience as well as in love.

And note this – man is made on the same day as the
animal world. Have you noticed that? In one sense, he is
an animal, made out of dust (2:7), mortal. Only God has
immortality, and in that sense man is like the animals. But
oh, how different! Do you remember the verse in John's
Gospel – Genesis is always leading us to the New
Testament – in John 2:25, where he says that Jesus
'Himself knew what was in man'? He understood man
perfectly. The two stories follow, of Nicodemus and the

woman at the well. To Nicodemus He says 'You must be born again'; to the woman, 'God is Spirit.' Now if I'd been Jesus I would have reversed them. I would have talked theology with Nicodemus and told the prostitute at the well to be born again. But Jesus reversed the order because He knew that the best of man needed to be reborn and the worst of man could know God. He had that balanced view of man.

I am pushing this hard because I think that this is what Genesis is very much about. For those who think through these things, there are many things in psychology, philosophy and sociology – if you want to use those words – that hinge on whether or not man 'is'. I do not believe that we will understand the world until we recognise the biblical view of man – that he can respond to God, that he is made in His image; and yet that all men, because they are dust, and because of Genesis 3, are sinners in need of redemption.

Thirdly, *a completed work*. The first three verses of chapter 2 are one of those lovely moments in the Bible. I hope that when you read your Bible you wait for the unexpected (I have found some dull things in the world, but never Bible study!). When I get to these verses I am waiting for something. 'There was evening and there was morning', we read, 'the first . . . second . . . third . . . fourth . . . fifth . . . sixth day . . .' I read the first three verses about the seventh day and I wait for it . . . and it isn't there! 'There was evening and there was morning – the seventh day' – have you got that in your Bibles? If so, get rid of that Bible! It is not there. It has not ended, we are still living in the seventh day; it is the world in which we live.

This tells us two great things. God has, in one sense, finished His work. It is completed. But that does not mean, secondly, that God is passive and inactive and has gone to sleep. No: Jesus said, 'My Father is working and I am working still' (John 5:17). The work is finished and we can rejoice in it; there would be no science if that were not true – but our God is still at work. The double message is, thank God for His completed work, His finished work in Jesus which is linked in Scripture with this; thank God for that Sabbath rest into which we can all enter, of which the Epistle to the Hebrews speaks; but also, there is something said about the rhythm of work and rest. The Sabbath day is very important. It is interesting that the Commandments link on to this. Some people say that we have no right to tell non-Christians they must have a day of rest and worship on Sundays, that it's got nothing to do with how they live. But I think it has. It's not just a Christian ordinance, it's a creation ordinance. Even Christians these days play fast and loose with the day of the Lord, so I think we should watch it! A preacher once told me that he had never taken a day off over a very long period. And then he was ill and confined to bed for a long period. He had his Sabbath rest. I believe we flaunt God's law at our peril. How our nations needs to find that balance of work and rest that God fashioned! He has made us that way. We cannot go against that creation ordinance – this is God's world.

### This is man's world

Now the other question: what is man? I am going to say three things about man.

#### Man's unique position

What does it mean in 1:26, that man was made in God's image, in His likeness?

Does it not mean supremely that man is made with the quality of God, that he is able to choose? He may choose to worship, or not; he may respond to God, or reject Him. And we shall see as we proceed that he chose the way of rebellion. Why did God make us like that? Is it because He wanted us to love Him? You can make a robot do lots of things, but you cannot make it love you. You would not want to, because love is a choice, a free choice of a willing agent, and man was made that way. If you would turn to 9:6, the phrase 'made in the image of God' comes once more in our chapters, in a very significant place which we will look at from another angle later. But just notice: 'Whoever sheds the blood of man, by man shall his blood be shed' – for 'God made man in His own image.' The writer is saying quite simply that you must treat man as ultimately responsible; he cannot back out and say that murder was not his fault. He must be treated as a responsible person made in the image of God.

There is so much involved here. The whole idea of who man is, his unique position in God's world. I get worried about some people who seem more concerned about the animal world than the human world. However wonderful an animal might be, it does not worship God, it does not choose. But you do!

## Man's moral responsibility

In 1:28, God says to man, 'You must have dominion' – you are in charge. This is important. What a mess we have made of that responsibility! I remember George Hoffman of Tear Fund giving a moving address on the problem of suffering. Who better to talk, than a man who has witnessed suffering that 99.9% of us will never see? One of the things he said was that the vast majority of suffering is the direct result of man's inhumanity to man; the wars, the selfishness, the greed. Think of the mess man has made of the world from greed, the dust-bowls of our world; that is the biggest problem of suffering. Man was given charge, and left in charge.

Do you sometimes wonder, as I do, why God does not stop it? I have been recently very upset, more than usual, by the dreadful things happening in Beirut. I'm not getting involved in politics; but when I saw all that slaughter my heart wept, and I who weep very little physically almost wept when I watched it all and saw the kids in hospital. I want to say to God: Why do you not stop it? Is there a God, if He allows all this to go on?

Yet is it not true, that God has made man and left him in charge? He will not take away man's responsibility. Of course He does intervene sometimes, He does marvellously change things, as we all know; but if every time there was suffering and strife God stopped it, man would be man no more.

Let me give you two further scriptures. James 3:7,8; man has tamed everything 'but no human being can tame the tongue.' That is a sobering thought. And Romans 8:19-23, where Paul says that the whole creation is groaning and travailing, waiting for the day of redemption. We have injected sin into our world. Man will go on being greedy until he is gloriously redeemed.

## Man's vital relationships

In chapter 2, verse 4 onwards, the writer enlarges the picture of man, like a photographer enlarging a photograph. He tells us three things about the vital relationships of man.

*His relationship with his Lord.* God 'breathed into his nostrils the breath of life' (2:7) – so man has that unique relationship with his Lord. A similar verse is Job 32:8 – the 'breath of the Almighty' makes man what he is. I do hope that, as good biblical scholars, you know that it's not that man has a soul; he is a soul. That is why Christians care about body and mind as well as spirit. Man became a living soul with a unique relationship with his Lord.

There are some verses we sometimes leave out. In 2:8,9 and 2:15-17 we read that God put man in a garden. There man was given right from the start a choice; he had to decide. He was given a law: 'You can eat of every tree in the garden, but not of the tree of knowledge of good and evil.' Do you see, from the beginning man was given a place of testing? We often think of the garden of Eden as beautiful – no problems, perpetual sunshine, just walking with the Lord – marvellous! But there was work in the garden. That is what man was made for (verse 15). And in that garden, man had a responsibility to choose either to obey or not. The law is positive – 'You may eat . . .'; but there are limits, and the law of God is the most marvellous safeguard.

Man in his relationship with his Lord. If you break that relationship you cease to be man. I believe that a man who is not in touch with God through Jesus Christ is not fully man. He is dead in the most vital relationship of his life. I wonder if you believe that? If you did, Genesis would send you out in evangelism. Do you really believe that your neighbour – nice, pleasant, getting on well, fine and healthy – is really spiritually dead because he does not know Jesus? I guess if we all believed that, there would be a new surge for evangelism.

In 3:8 there is the best definition of what happened in that relationship. 'They heard the sound of the Lord God walking in the cool of the day.' Isn't that lovely? They had walked together, God and man. And we may do it again in Jesus.

*Man's vital relationship with his environment.* Time is beating me; let me just point out to you chapter 2 verses 4-6 and 10-14. It is a picture of a world to be enjoyed. God wants you to enjoy it. Christians are not hair-shirt, miserable people. God has not taken all the joy out of life. Some people live as if being a Christian were drab and dull. No! It is a world to be enjoyed, to be loved; and culture is to be used.

*The relationship between man and woman.* You get the picture (1:27) that from the beginning man was made male and female – equally man. Then in 2:18-25 you get the lovely 'blowing up' of that relationship. Did you notice that the first bit of poetry in the Bible was written when man found his mate? I am sure you did. Verse 23 is poetry.

It is a precious relationship. It is the devil's big battle-ground today – he really wants to destroy us, and he knows that if he can destroy this beautiful relationship he is doing very well. If your church does not have this as one of its problems, it is a marvellous church! It's happening everywhere.

There are three things that are marvellous about the relationship between man and woman. First, it is *a complementary relationship*. Note the phrase in verses 18 and 20, 'a helper fit for him'. It literally means, a help opposite him. That is why all extreme Women's Lib, all extreme male arrogance (and it's still there), is not Christian. We are heirs together; we belong to each other. Please, do not let the world con you by telling you that if there is any difference between the sexes it means you are inferior. That's nonsense! God bless the difference! It's why He made us.

Secondly, it is *an exclusive relationship*. Jesus, in Mark 10:8,9, quotes verse 24 in His inspired words about marriage. It is the exclusiveness of a lasting relationship between one man and one woman. Monogamy. It is the essence of creation. Do not believe the books that tell you it started with polygamy and only later became monogamy. It was the other way round. Yes, I know the problems that the Bible refers to in some cases – divorce, yes, I know all that! But the divine order is one man, one woman, for life. It means that a man must leave his father and mother. It is a practical thing; some parents will not let their children leave; honestly, some of the biggest problems in marriage are the parents of those who are married.

And – please – no leaving without cleaving. Marriage is to be exclusive, for ever. I am sure that there are some who have already sinned in that respect. It is not an unforgiveable sin; God is merciful; but it is still a sin. If any are leaving without cleaving, and are trying to justify it in Scripture – forget it! Because you will never do so. Come clean!

Some years ago I dared to preach on the Song of Solomon (I always maintained that a man should not preach on the Song of Solomon until he is fifty years old – it is beyond the understanding of anybody younger – but I prejudged it by a year or two!). I believe that it is not just about a relationship between a person and Jesus, it is about a relationship betweeen a man and a woman. (I think it has a lot to do with sexual relationships, but that is by the way.) 4:12 is a great verse: 'A garden locked is my sister, my bride.' Then in verse 16, 'Let my beloved come to his garden.'

If I speak to some who long that the garden may be unlocked to somebody – keep it locked, until that somebody comes; do not imagine that you are going to get fulfilment and joy by unlocking to an illicit relationship. It is desperately relevant, terribly important; it is exclusive.

And finally, it is *an innocent relationship*. Chapter 2 ends as beautifully as chapter 1: man and his wife in the garden, both naked and not ashamed. Why did the church at one time give the impression that somehow all sexual relationships were, if not bad, at least not talked about? Why did it get frightened of sex? Sex is a beautiful gift of God, given in creation. He wants husband and wife to enjoy all its beauty.

It was innocent. But, you will know, because you have read chapter 3 before, that almost the first casualty of sin was that they saw they were naked, and were ashamed. I make no apology for ending on that note. I believe it may be the battle-ground even beyond scientific origins and all the rest of these chapters. If God through these days speaks to some of us, and helps us to recapture something of the beauty of the relationship between man and wife – man and woman in God's plan – then it will all be worthwhile.

In our next study we see the other side of man. Thank God today that paradise has not altogether been lost, and thank God supremely that there was a day when, in another garden, a second Adam came to fight the fight — and you and I can once more enjoy what man was meant to be.

# 2. Sin in God's World
# (Genesis 3)

Just one chapter: but what a terribly important chapter, as we see sin in God's world! I suggest to you that if the third chapter of Genesis had never been written, somebody would have had to write it; for you cannot understand the world without it. Far from being an embarrassment, the doctrine of original sin is, for me, the only way to explain the strange world in which we live and the strange phenomenon which is mankind. There is for example no doubt that we must take Genesis 3 as historical narrative, otherwise you are left with many very real problems. One of the things about these first eleven chapters is the way they almost (not entirely) get lost for the rest of the Old Testament, and then suddenly become a very important part of the New. Paul picks up the great picture of Adam and Christ in Romans 5:18,19: one man's trespass, one man's righteousness; one man's disobedience, one man's obedience. I don't think I'm being unduly simplistic, but if you take away the historicity of Adam, you are left with very real problems about the reality of Christ. 1 Corinthians 15:20-22; 'As in Adam all die, so in Christ shall all be made alive.' Just as Christ is the head of the new humanity, so Adam is of the old.

So here we are in the real history of yesterday's world, but with a history that is relevant today. Adam is, in another sense, you and me. I hope somewhere in our study you'll hear God saying, 'You are the man . . . you are the woman . . .' Just one more word about historicity. It seems to me obvious that you have got to take Satan very seriously. He, also, is a significant figure in this chapter. If you are going to try to understand the world, and you rule out Satan, I believe you are making an awful mistake as well as denying the truth of Scripture. 'The serpent was more subtle than any other creature,' says verse 1 of our chapter, and so he is, and one of his subtleties is to persuade some people that he doesn't exist. He must be delighted when he hears clever folk denying his existence! He also wants folk to get caught up in sensationalist satanic interest; and there is nothing he loves more than when the cnurch concentrates, with a desperate thirst for sensationalism, on the periphery of Satan.

Oh yes; there *are* demons. But Satan worked in the garden in a much more subtle way than with demons. Years ago, a student asked me to cast out from her a demon of laziness. I told her I would do no such thing, but that I would give her some good advice on how to get up in the morning and pray. She went out very disappointed. She didn't want that much demand made on her. She wanted a demon cast out. There was no demon of laziness in her. Satan is subtle; and what she needed was to guard against the kind of thing that we will find in this tremendously important chapter. It's what Satan is always doing. If you want to understand Satan and man – here's your chapter.

Just one more thing in preparation. We see in this chapter what I call the other face of man. Let us hold on to it; in Genesis 1 and 2 we saw that man is made in the image of God; don't leave that behind. Man is a wonderful creation. But there is the other side.

Sometimes man does things so wonderful that you can

understand why the Psalmist says in Psalm 8:5, 'You have made him a little less than divine.' He is almost like God! But there are also times when man is worse than the beasts. A French philosopher called him 'the glory and the scum of the universe.' Quite right. There is a Jekyll and a Hyde in the heart of all of us. I remember one New Year I was lying in bed and I turned on the radio for the first news bulletin of the year; and as I heard the first two items, it was Genesis 3 all over again. The first was that amazing miracle, the first heart transplant in South Africa. The second concerned Vietnam, where the truce had broken yet again and man was slaughtering man. I said to myself: isn't that a parable? Man can give a new physical heart, but he cannot tame himself spiritually. And what Genesis says to you, to me, to many misguided people in our world, who care about our world, is: 'You will never put the world right until you put man right.'

Of course we care about the environment. Of course we care about social issues. But the Christian believes that the heart of man's problems is man himself; and we need to understand that, if we are going to change society. To try to do so without understanding Genesis 3 is to waste the time of many good but misguided people. So we turn now to Genesis 3, and just so that you will know that there is hope, even in that chapter, I will tell you that we will finish at verse 15. It is a great note of gospel hope. It is there – wait for it!

## Man falling (Genesis 3:1-13)

We will consider the chapter under two headings, man falling, and man fallen; how it happened, and what came of it. And first,

### Sin conceived (verses 1-5)
'The devil,' said Jesus, in John 8:44, 'is the father of lies'; and Satan begins his great act in our world by insinuating

into the minds of the man and the woman the thought that God is not true.

Now please note; if you read Isaiah 14:12-15 you can read about the fall of Satan. He wanted to ascend, he wanted to be like God. He wasn't content to be an angel, he wanted to be as great as God Himself, and so he fell.

Have you noticed that such is sin, when somebody falls from grace they always want to drag somebody else with them? You know, when I was a boy playing cricket and I was got out without scoring any runs, I longed for somebody in the team to do as badly. When they did I felt a little bit happier, because then they were as bad as I was. I knew it wasn't right, but I kept on thinking that way because, you see, you want to drag somebody down with you. And Satan who wanted primacy had fallen; and he insinuates to Adam and Eve, 'Don't you want to be like God?' and he brings them down, like he was himself brought down.

Notice also, how this sin was conceived. The serpent was subtle. 2 Corinthians 2:11; 'We are not ignorant of his devices.' Sadly, lots of Christians are. He's subtle – so watch. 2 Corinthians 11:3: 'I am afraid,' says Paul, 'that as the serpent deceived Eve by his cunning, your thoughts will be led astray from a sincere and pure devotion to Christ.' It wasn't, in one sense, a frontal attack; there was no terribly wicked sin in the garden of Eden, nothing that would get headline revelations in the newspapers today. Nothing like that. A reporter would be hard pressed to find anything terribly awful about Genesis 3 – and yet, it was the beginning of sin.

What did he insinuate? Note verse 3: '*Did* God say?' – 'Is it *really* true?' Now notice, here's Satan's way. First of all, doubt in God's Word. Second, disbelief at God's Word. Thirdly, disobedience to God's Word. I want to say to you at Keswick that one of the greatest dangers of our day is not this that or the other sin, but the diminishing of the authority of God's Word. Everything else flows from that. The moment you do not have God's Word as your final authority, anything can rush in. Of course it can. We don't call sinful the things the Bible calls sinful any more. We've shut our Bibles. It's not just liberal theologians who are closing their Bibles today. Some misguided evangelicals believe that they have a sort of hot line from heaven, that they don't need God's Word any more; and it's dangerous, terribly dangerous; beware! Read a bit of church history. When the Bibles get shut it only takes a year or two for the Bible to be denied. If Satan puts doubts into your mind about the authority of Scripture, say 'Get behind me, Satan,' open your Bible, and keep it open.

And they, you see, by verse 4 the serpent will flatly contradict God's Word, the moment he has got into the thought-life. The moment he has insinuated the possibility that God's Word might not be true, he says, 'You won't die.' Verse 5: 'I tell you,' says Satan, 'God's a great spoilsport.' Oh, Satan loves to tell you that! 'You'll be fulfilled if you disobey God's word.'

Now here's the crunch question. Who was right? Satan, or God? Glance on to verse 7. What happened when Adam and Eve disobeyed? Did they die? Did they know like God? It's very interesting; it seems, at first, that Satan was right. They didn't die physically. They were still very much alive. And what happened? 'The eyes of both were opened and they knew they were naked' – and in a sense Satan *was* right. Oh, he is subtle. What happened was that they had a bizarre knowledge; their fulfilment led them into that strange end of innocence.

Have we grasped this, that the mark of sin conceived is disobedience? The Bible keeps on saying, 'sin is rebellion', 'sin is disobedience'. It is easy at Keswick to be very aware of the sins of our society. It is very important that we should be reminded of that, and those sins are partly our responsibility; but ultimately, sin is disobedience, and it could well be that some of us here

stand before God even more guilty because we hear God's
law and we say 'No'.

## Sin born (verses 6 and 7)

Once the thought had been put first into the mind of Eve,
thought led to action; and that action involved others. You
can never sin to yourself. Always your sin involves
somebody else, like a ripple on water. How often we've
found, in our own lives and in our pastoral ministry, that
God forgives, and He can restore, but you can't take the
ripples back. The effect of that sin will often go on for
years and years after you've been restored and forgiven.
It's marvellous that you have been; but there's a kind of
cheap grace talked about nowadays which suggests that
because the God of forgiveness can work even through
your sinful disobedience to bring you back to Him, it's
almost good that you have sinned! – no, no, no.
Somebody else, hurt along the way, might not so easily get
back to God. Sin always involves others. Verse 6 is a classic
illustration of 1 John 2:16 – the lust of the flesh, the lust of
the eyes, the pride of life. You can sum up sin very easily in
those three categories. The woman saw that it was good for
food, that it was a delight to the eyes, and to make one
wise.

One other thing: Eve was attracted, in a strange way,
because of an insatiable curiosity in the heart of man and
woman. They had been told (2:15-17) that they could eat
of any tree – but not that one. And that was the test of
mankind. Now, let's be honest; isn't that true of all of us?
If you've children you'll know that you've only to say to
them 'You must not go into that place' to make them want
to go there. Sometimes you even allow for it. If you don't
want them to do it, you tell them that they must do it – and
they won't! It is very important to recognise that in the
heart of all people is that which cannot go the right way. It
was St Augustine's realisation that 'thou shalt not'
immediately made him want to do the forbidden thing,

that convinced him he was a sinner. Or, read Romans 7 and the story of Paul.

Go a step further, and note the absolute simplicity of the step that brought sin into the world. All it says is 'She took . . . she ate.' As simple as that; and yet, in a sense, upon that primal act of disobedience hinged all that has happened in our world. You see, the greatest moments to fear are not when you face some obvious temptation and the devil comes like a roaring lion; they're the simple things, just every day acts. (I'm indebted to Derek Kidner – whose commentary I have recommended to you – for pointing out that it's the exact parallel of the simple thing that Jesus, the second Adam, did in the upper room, when He said to the disciples, 'Take and eat'. But the lovely thought is that you can get back as simply, in that sense, as you went out.) So I want to remind you that the temptations that face you are not only the big ones; you've got to walk in tune with God all the time. Eve 'took and ate', and sin was born, and verse 7 happened: 'then the eyes of them both were opened.' I mentioned at the end of our last study that the sex relationship, one of the most beautiful things in God's economy, was the first thing to go wrong. Very important. The devil knows where to start. They haven't committed any sexual sin, but all at once they see that what before was innocent was now shot through with sinfulness.

Why? Titus 1:15; 'To the pure all things are pure, but to the believing and corrupt mind, nothing is pure.' So they projected into that lovely thing God had given them the sinfulness of their heart and from that moment on the relationship was spoiled. You've only got to pick up any newspaper, any day – not just the dramatic headlines – to see how many sins start with the misuse of sex.

## Sin discovered (verses 8-13)

Ponder that lovely picture in verse 8. 'They heard the sound of the Lord God walking in the garden in the cool of

the day.' Some commentators call this an 'anthropo-
morphism'. That means, God is seen in terms of man.
Previous verses have talked about the hands of God and
the eyes of God and here it talkes about God walking in the
garden in the cool of the day.

You can explain that in all sorts of ways. I don't know
whether they really saw the form of the Lord God walking
with them. I really don't; it's one of those 'secret things
that belong to the Lord our God'. A man once complained
to me that he wished the story of creation had been written
in scientific language, then he would have found it easier.
Oh, how glad I am that it wasn't! For now every one of us
can understand. You see, you can have an artist come to
paint a picture of your wife, or you can go to the local
hospital and get an X-ray of her insides; but I imagine the
one you'd hang up over the mantelpiece would be the
artist's painting (and I dare suggest that it would be the
truer of the two as well – but that's another matter).

The Lord God was walking in the garden in the cool of
the day. The relationship was close. We see it again with
Enoch and Noah. Don't say, 'It's the Old Testament, they
were a long way away from a great and awesome and
terrible God.' They walked with God. And when you come
back to Christ, you begin to walk with God again. Oh, I
love that verse 8!

But it wasn't lovely, was it. At the end of the verse, 'the
man and his wife hid themselves from the presence of the
Lord God' in the trees of the garden. They wanted to get
away. In Revelation 6:16 you may read that on the final
day of judgement 'people will say on that day, "Hide
us"' – they'll call on the rocks to hide them from the wrath
of the Lamb. They shall know that they cannot stand
before Him. Ah, but Revelation 22:4 says, 'They shall see
His face.' Parents: don't you know when your children
have done something they oughtn't to have done? They
don't look you in the eye. When the eyes are lowered you
say 'What's up? What's gone wrong?' I gather it happens

between husband and wife sometimes too. They can't look each other in the eye. Man could not look God in the eye; something had gone wrong. He wanted to hide.

Now note – it's very important – what was God's first word to sinful man. Not a condemnation; not a command; but a question. 'Adam, where are you?'

When Cain sinned, what did God do with Cain at that moment? He asked him three questions. 4:6, 'Why are you angry?'; 4:9, 'Where is Abel your brother?'; and 4:10, 'What have you done?' Let me bring in two others. Jesus' first word to Paul on the Damascus road: 'Saul, why do you persecute me?' And to a man who is possessed by demons, His question is 'What is your name?' You see, what God does, what Jesus was doing, is always to treat our freedom seriously. He will not force us. He will not drive us. We are not robots. We must respond in love. And He wants us to find out where we are. I think it says to those of use who preach, that our job is to draw people to that place where they will recognise their need, not force it, willy-nilly, into them.

In my own call to the ministry, what turned me inside out was that haunting question in Isaiah 6, when God said to Isaiah – not 'Go' – but 'Whom shall I send and who will go for us?' And at Keswick you are being asked questions. 'Where are you?' – 'Where do you stand in relation to me?' – 'How do you walk with me?'

Adam's answer in verse 10 is a very revealing one. He's all mixed up inside. He reveals that he is actually already separated by sin in his own heart. 'I heard the sound – and I was afraid.' This fear complex is very strange, isn't it? Most people are frightened of something or somebody. There is an awful timidity around, a fearfulness; and here is sin making Adam mixed up and fearful inside. So God draws him out further, in verse 11. 'Who told you you were naked? Have you eaten of the tree which I commanded you not to eat?' Ah, poor Adam. He answered the first but he didn't answer the second, because what he wanted to do was to pass the buck. Have you noticed, that if a man does something good – it's his own achievement; 'I did it!' But if he does something wrong – 'Well, it's not really my fault, it was the wife' – or something else, our genes or our heredity or our environment. You know, when I congratulate somebody who's done well in exams they don't normally say 'Well, it was my genes, it was my clever grandfather – nothing to do with me!' They usually bow their heads in reticence and accept the praise.

How often we pass the buck, when it's a matter of sin. And, if I may say so with all seriousness, that's the problem in our society. We've grown up with this big con, that ultimately it's nobody's fault. I know we do take heredity and background into account, but I've been a pastor for twenty-five years and I have seen people with identical backgrounds going in directly opposite ways; I can think of a person who ought logically to be a menace to society yet is a wonderful gift of God's grace, and somebody with every advantage of background who is a menace to society. There is within all of us a responsibility that we finally have to take. Once you remove that, you are not man or woman any more.

And so God tried to draw Adam out, but Adam is not there yet. He is man, falling.

## Man fallen (Genesis 3:14-24)

And this is what results from man's fall. What happened in that garden in the East and what happens today in this garden in the West is all the same.

### The story of suffering (verses 14-19)

If you want to push me on the point – I think I do believe that the serpent really did crawl before this moment. But that's not the important thing. The important thing is the verdict on woman and man in verses 16-19.

I think it is idle to speculate 'I wonder what it would have been like if Adam and Eve had never fallen . . . Would there never have been any physical suffering? Would they have remained in the garden alone for ever?' We have no idea, so let's leave that with the secret things. I'm not prepared to waste time arguing about things that neither you nor I know. But one thing we do know. They sinned, and because they sinned, suffering came.

Verse 16: it affected the sex relationship. There we are again; it affected the birth of children. I don't know whether an unfallen Eve could have had painless childbirth, but I do know what verse 16 is saying. In that relationship, instead of joy and freedom and liberation came pain, instinct and domination; and that is one result of sin.

Then in verse 17, work becomes a drudgery. This is happening so much in our society today. How do we redeem this whole idea of work, and cope with the whole business of unemployment? How is it possible for people to say that whatever job they do, they do it as to the Lord? (In my job it's easy, of course!) I remember one lady's testimony; she was a lavatory assistant, and I remember her telling how much difference it made, being a Christian. I was very moved by that. She did it as to the Lord. We are living in a world where it is not easy, is it? Work is important – and I think that if it is important that there should be one day's rest in seven then it's equally important that there should be hard work in the rest of the week; but work has been vitiated by sin. 'Cursed is the ground because of you, in toil shall you eat of it all the days of your life'. Work, that was meant to be a privilege, will become a toil and a drudgery, and all the time that world you work in is infected by sin, as Paul reminds us in Romans 8:18 onwards. He talks about thorns and thistles; and if you study thorns and thistles in Scripture you will see that they are a symbol of God's judgement on man. Here's a picture of work vitiated by sin and a whole world soured.

One last thing in the story of suffering. Not only home relationships suffer, not only work, but also the very facts of man's mortality. 'Dust you are, to dust you shall return.' Ultimately, across all of our lives, death casts its shadow. Here we know that we are mortal; and oh, that we may live in the light of it! With all God's grace, I am mortal, I am dust. Don't you love that psalm which says 'He remembers that we are but dust'? Can I remind any status-seeking people, that there is one common thing about all of us? Unless Christ returns before we die, we all go the same way. Every one of us. People won't acknowledge it; they honestly think that although they brought nothing into this world, they're going to take something out. Oh yes, they've made their name. But I have to tell you with great sadness, that I have taken funeral services for people of great distinction, and I had nothing to say except a few trite words; that they had been important in some job. And all I could do was then to preach the gospel and hope that some would repent. Oh yes; to dust you return. That's the story of suffering. That's the other side of man.

## The story of separation (verses 22-24)
Already separated and hiding from God, man is now separated for ever. You see the real separation we're dealing with is between God and man. Of course we're concerned about the separation between man and man. But we can only bring colour, background and class together when we bring people to God. Between verses 22 and 24 there is a very solemn picture of a final separation from God. Adam and Eve chose the way of sin; so they were cast out. They couldn't walk with the Lord in the garden any more; they were outside. You can see from verse 24 that there was no way back, and from that moment on right through the Old Testament, everything said 'No way back'. The temple was full of separation. The gentiles, the women, all but the high priest kept out of

there; and the veil was pierced only once a year, covered with the blood of bulls and goats. And isn't it marvellous, that on the day that Jesus died the veil was rent in two, and He said to the penitent thief, 'Today . . . in Paradise.' The garden of Eden again. Hebrews 10:19-22 undergirds it: we live the other side of the rent veil – but there could only be a rent veil because Jesus died. Let us never forget that by nature we are outside, and by nature there is no way through.

One little note: observe the cherubim in verse 24. In the Old Testament the cherubim were very much around the veil and the ark of the covenant, like God's guardian angels keeping the way back to God. Not until we take this seriously will we take the gospel seriously. After all, if a man is not doomed to perish without Christ, what does John 3:16 mean? There's no gospel any more. There's no gift of eternal life. So we must take this very seriously; rejoice that we are on the other side, and pray for many who have not yet found their way back.

### The story of salvation (verse 15)
Now here's the good news! Just before we look at verse 15, look at verse 20. Adam gives his wife a name of hope. 'Eve' means 'living'. What a moment to give a wife a name like that! But, there's hope.

There are those who will read into verse 21 the story of the atonement. May I stick my neck out? Do be careful with fanciful interpretations. I don't really think you can press the verse to say that God clothing them with garments is a symbol of our need to be clothed in His righteousness alone, though that need is a real one. I do however believe that verse 21 reminds us that God doesn't leave sinful man out in the cold. He hasn't stopped caring for Adam just because He has thrown him out. When Cain murders his brother God doesn't leave him to his own deserts. He's still caring for him; isn't that wonderful? Long before you were converted, God was watching over you. He didn't leave you, and He doesn't leave that world to which we've got to return.

Back to verse 15, and here's the great gospel message. Let's just pick out a few choice thoughts. Notice, that this word of hope springs from the very sentence of God. At the moment He judges man, He gives him a hope. I think a lot of us have the idea that man was put in the garden, and God *hoped* that he would always walk with Him, and then it went wrong, and God had to think, 'What on earth am I going to do?' No. He had already planned it; the Lamb, slain from before the foundations of the world. It was already there, in God's eternal plan. Don't press me further; we're back in the 'secret things'; but I just praise God. I think it's marvellous to think that way back in the eternal counsels His plan was being formulated. And what was the plan? Verse 15: 'He shall bruise your head [serpent], and you shall bruise His heel.'

It speaks of somebody born of a woman; not, I believe, a reference to a virgin birth, though that fits and I happily believe it; but it's really saying that a person born into this world, descended from sinful Adam, would ultimately bruise the head of the serpent. That person would win; but it would be costly. In Galatians 3:16 the 'seed' is Christ. He is the seed of Abraham, of Adam; and in Him comes the fulfilment. He defeats Satan, He bruises the serpent's head, but in the process He dies.

There's your atonement. There it is. 'Within a garden secretly, and on the cross on high' – the second Adam took our sin, not just Adam's sin but all our sin, and there defeated the evil one. Amen!

But I have just one last lovely thing for you. In some Bibles Genesis 3:16 is cross-referenced to that remarkable verse Romans 16:20. Paul's final word to the church at Rome is this: 'The God of peace will shortly crush Satan under your feet.' Now that is one of the moments when I really feel like shouting 'Hallelujah!' It's marvellous. He says, not

'Christ's feet', but 'your feet'; and here's the wonder of
the gospel of salvation. The church is the body of Christ;
and we can expect to see the victory of the cross being
worked out in our lives and our fellowship. We need not
live in defeat, with all this being true; salvation grows right
out of the heart of suffering and separation and sin. That's
wonderful! And we can see it worked out, in our lives.

# 3. Death in God's World
# (Genesis 4-11)

In these chapters we see how the sin that we saw in Genesis 3 begins to spiral. But lest you become very heavy-hearted, can I remind you that alongside the spiralling of sin and death comes also the great message of God's grace. 'Where sin increased grace abounded all the more,' says Romans 5:20, a divine commentary upon these chapters. For example in chapter 5, with its repeating refrain 'And he died . . . and he died . . . and he died', right in the middle – verse 24 – comes a glorious beam of light. You wait for the refrain and it's not there: 'Enoch walked with God, and he was not, for God took him.'

And when we come to the flood, and we see the note of God's judgement, we'll see that at the moment of greatest judgement comes the moment of greatest hope; and when we see the Tower of Babel in ruins, thank God, out of the ashes of the tower steps Abraham, the great man of faith.

Well now, if our last study, the story of sin, was the story of Satan's activity, there is a danger nevertheless of blaming it all on Satan. Don't forget, he can only work if you and I allow him. He is not sovereign in our lives. In a sense he disappears in these chapters – apart from the very vivid metaphor in 7:4, 'Sin is crouching at the door.' It's a

picture of a wild animal waiting to pounce. Says God:
'You must master it.' It can be done. But instead of Satan
being in the centre, the world begins to be central; and the
world brings death.

So there are two halves to our study, following on from
our last: 'Sin grown' and 'Sin judged'.

## Sin grown (chapters 4-6)

Of course there are intriguing question-marks over
chapter 4. And, if you ask me in 5:17 who was Cain's wife,
I've got a simple answer. I've no idea. I don't know who he
married. Certainly 4:14 suggests that the world was already
populated, and it may be that God did create other
'Adams' while there were Adam and Eve; but we don't
know, so we leave it there, in the secret things of God. But
the chapter is not a chapter about 'Where did all those
people come from?' and 'Who was Cain's wife?' It is all to
do with you and me. It's interesting; Cain and Abel
disappear after chapter 4 until the New Testament. 1 John
3:12 makes a comment about Cain. Why did he murder his
brother? Because his own deeds were evil and his brother's
righteous. He appears again in Jude 11. In Hebrews 11:4
Abel is seen as a man of faith. And then in a marvellous
verse, 12:24, it talks about the blood of Jesus, the mediator
of a new covenant, speaking more graciously than the
blood of Abel. Abel's blood cries for vengeance. The
blood of Jesus cries for pardon.

What is the dominant thought in your mind when you
think of evil men? Is the cry 'Vengeance', or is it 'Mercy'?
I was in Northern Ireland a few weeks ago, and met a
young man, now a minister in the Presbyterian Church in
Northern Ireland, whose call to the ministry hinged on the
murder of his brother by the IRA. This was his testimony.
'I'd either got to become like them and spend my life in
bitterness and hatred and revenge, or do something to
change the climate with a message of love.' I believe that

this is where the message of Cain and Abel is right up to date. It's very easy for us in Keswick far from grim events, to see how these chapters apply to men of violence; but I want to remind you that it was Jesus who said that if we plot murder in our hearts, if we speak words of hatred with our lips, *we* are murderers. The message of Cain is not just a message to the few who happen to have murdered their brothers. It's a message to all of us.

*Sin growing*

It starts with spoiled relationships. What went wrong? It's particularly sad because we can look at verse 1, when Cain is born and there is the lovely comment, 'I have gotten a man with the help of the Lord.' That's a nice phrase, isn't it? Here was hope for the future. Yet Cain was such a tragic disaster. And what happened in those spoiled relationships? How did that sin grow? Well, notice first, *The cause of hatred (4:1-7)*. Here we're going deep. Satan is never more active than when we're involved in religious things. The whole problem of Cain and Abel came to a head when they both offered their sacrifices. They both came to God, they were both involved in worship; and at that point the seed of murder was sown in the heart of Cain because of that awful sin of envy, as old as man and as young as man.

Why did God accept Abel's sacrifice and not Cain's? Why did He say, 'I like Abel's but I don't like Cain's'? It's quite simple. Not because Abel, with a great prophetic vision of the future, offered a sacrifice with blood in it, and Cain made the mistake of bringing a sacrifice from the ground. I believe that that makes Scripture less challenging than it ought to be. No; it was because Cain's religious activity was a cloak for his own sin. Proverbs 21:27, 'The sacrifice of the wicked is an abomination: how much more, when he brings it with evil intent.' Right through Scripture we are reminded by the prophets that people can be deeply involved in religious activities, worship in church, attendance at a convention – while their hearts are far from God. It doesn't mean, because you've come to Keswick, that you're walking close to God. Of course not. Many go into God's presence whose hearts are far away from Him. Isaiah 1:10 onwards: 'Why do you keep trampling my courts? Why do you keep lifting up your hands in your worship? I don't see them, because your hands are full of blood.'

People spend hours worrying about how we worship. God's not all that bothered about how we worship; but He's infinitely bothered about how we live. And because Cain was not right with God, and Abel was, one sacrifice was rejected and the other accepted, and this was where hatred began. Would you notice (verse 4) 'When the Lord had regard for Abel and his offering and not for Cain's, Cain was very angry, and his countenance fell.' Here's sin, isn't it? In a sense Cain might have been happy if neither sacrifice had been accepted, but he was envious because Abel's was and his was not. And envy began to lead into hatred.

You would be a strange person if you had never almost wished that some people were not as saintly as they are. Oh yes, some of us have been greatly helped by saintly people – but aren't there moments when we're almost delighted to discover that even the saints have feet of clay? John says that when the light came into the world, people preferred darkness rather than light, because their deeds were evil. The very goodness of Abel and the acceptance of his sacrifice drove Cain down.

One other thing: God was going to have justice. Verse 10: 'The noise of your brother's blood is crying to me from the ground.' God is a God of justice. Forgiveness isn't pretending it did not happen; there can only be forgiveness if you believe in justice. But it goes further. God wants to stop Cain before hatred becomes murder and He asks him the question you see in verses 6 and 7. 'Why? Why?' But Cain rejects Him. There's the cause of hatred.

Please be honest about your envy. Some sins we confess rather more easily than others, and the sin of envy is one of the most difficult ones. I guess it is riddling the churches of our land. We find it hard to rejoice, when they've been blessed and we haven't. We find it hard to accept that that church down the road is full and overflowing and we seem to be bashing our head against a brick wall. The devil wants to get in with envy. At that point the Lord says, 'Why? Don't you trust me?'

*The consequences of hatred (4:8-14).* Note the way it goes; it's still so true. When God tried to plead with Cain the effect was that he actually went in the opposite direction (4:8) and murdered his brother. I've often thought, it's so much like Jesus and Judas. When Jesus gave Judas the sop at the eleventh hour to draw him back from his wicked act, the very fact of Jesus' graciousness only made Judas' sin all the worse. He was trying to draw Judas back, but, says John, in those awesome monosyllables, 'Judas went out and it was night.' If you come to a point where God is speaking to you about that in your life which is making you bitter, then if you don't respond you go out into the night. You are worse than you were when you came in, for if you reject the light, you walk into the night.

Then come the three questions to Cain: 'Why . . .? Where . . .? What . . .?' And when He asks the question 'Where?' in verse 9, there comes that famous rhetorical counter-question, 'Am I my brother's keeper?'

Now I want to say to you, 'Yes; you are.' Well, you know that, don't you? But you are responsible for your brother. It's no good saying, 'I'm not responsible for what happens to him.'

We're moved when people are killed in our own streets by acts of violence. But are we moved when thousands die in foreign streets, thousands of miles away? Do we weep for the millions who die of starvation? Are we righteously indignant when essential workers go on strike, and yet withhold giving to the refugee needs of the world, where people die in their millions? I believe that the Lord is saying to us that we are our brother's keeper. Not to go out from Keswick in caring love, doing all we can, means that we are as irresponsible as Cain. And you will notice that because of Cain's impenitence (verses 11 and 12) there is a greater judgement on Cain than upon Adam.

One further thing, and it does go further down. I'm sorry – we will be lifted up before we finish – but we're first going down even further. Verse 13 – do you notice? – Cain, in his impenitence, wants to argue with God. And one of the most awesome things about sin is that we disobey God very easily, and then we blame the consequences on Him. 'My punishment is greater than I can bear.' Some of the hardest times in the pastoral ministry are those spent trying to minister to people who will not only not repent of sin but want to blame other people for it. There is nothing more wonderful in the ministry than ministering to the penitent, and nothing more terrible than trying to minister to those who refuse to admit their responsibility.

Here's Cain. He's concerned about his well-being. He wants to blame God.

*The cure for hatred (verses 15 and 16).* But even Cain is going to be protected by God. God will not allow indiscriminate vengeance against Cain, and in verse 15 He can say that He is going to watch over him. Remember that. Isn't it wonderful? God doesn't leave sinners to their own fate, otherwise we'd be in a parlous state. And so Cain went away, into the land of Nod.

## Society infected

Note things that happen, from 4:17 to the end of the chapter and on into chapter 5. Verse 17: cities are built. Nothing wrong with that, city life is not wrong. Verse 21: music is born. Well, that's good, isn't it? Music is part of God's creation – lovely. Verse 22: industry begins. I've often thought of telling Sheffield City Council that their patron saint is Tubal-Cain. Well, all that's good, isn't it?

But I'm sure that at the end of this chapter, in verse 24, when Lamech uses industry for weapons of war, we've reached an important turning point. Just two things about that. There's nothing wrong with scientific progress; of course we must push the frontiers back. But it's what you do with what you discover that's the trouble. And please note the other thing, and the contrast in Old and New Testaments. Verse 24: Lamech says 'I've been avenged seventy-seven times, I've got my own back.' Does your mind link on to a New Testament passage here? Matthew 18:22: Peter says to Jesus, 'How often should I forgive my brother? Seven times?' And Jesus says, 'No, till seventy times seven.' One version says seventy-seven fold. You see the contrast? Lamech says, 'Vengeance seventy-seven times!' Jesus says, 'Forgiveness seventy-seven times!' No limits to forgiveness.

I don't find it easy. When I see bodies strewn around on the television news I have to battle not to want vengeance and murder in my heart. Do you know what I do then? I sing to myself that lovely song, 'Lord, make me a channel of your peace; where there is hatred let me bring your love.' That's what Jesus wants to say to us.

We go on into chapter 5 and society's still being infected. There's the monotonous repetition, 'And he died . . . and he died . . . and he died . . .' Now, do I believe that Methuselah lived to be 969, and that Enoch in verse 23 was a mere chicken of 365? Let's just say this. It is possible that the account of Seth, for example, is the account of a family line. It is possible, also, that they really did live longer lives. Or it may be that a year wasn't measured like it is today. Well, those are the secret things. I've told you the problem, and I don't really know the answer. But one thing I do know, whether you live to be 70 or 969; whether you live a short life or a massively long one; the phrase comes, 'and he died'. It's what Hebrews 2:15 calls 'man all his life long in fear because of the bondage of death.' It comes. You cannot finally cheat it. Remember it; society infected.

### The world condemned

Everything is now building up to the climax of the flood. In chapter 6 there are two sides, as we prepare for it and God's judgement on sin. Two things; first of all,

*Man's presumption (6:1-4).* It's quite a passage we're studying, full of exciting, interesting, controversial things. We do not know exactly what verse 1 means. Some say it refers to angels and men, others that it is two groups of men, one deriving from Cain the rejected, the other from Seth, the accepted. But what we do know is that it's the beginning of a great strand in Scripture which says that we must not be unequally yoked together with unbelievers.

Ours is a strangely liberated age; we all think we know better these days. One of the places where I think Christians need to go on sticking firm is here. There is no liberation from a divine principle, and if I flout it I can expect problems. Oh, I know what it's like. 'Oh, I know he's not a Christian and I know he doesn't come to church but I really believe he will, when we're married, if I persevere.' How often I have to take them through Scripture, graciously I hope, and say: God never guides you in contradiction with the clear teaching of His word. Oh, He may be kind to you; and though you disobey Him and rebel against Him you still may have a happy marriage, but you've no right to expect it. And this starts as early as Genesis 6.

And what I do know about Genesis 6, whatever may be this kind of relationship, is that there in verse 3 – this is man's presumption, man going his own way – there comes this awesome verse, 'My spirit shall not abide in man for ever, for he is flesh; but his day shall be one hundred and twenty years.' The last phrase might mean that he'll live a shorter life. It might mean God was going to be patient for yet another hundred and twenty years; what Peter talks about – God being patient in the days of Noah. But it's the first bit that's the awesome bit. 'My spirit shall not abide, or strive, in man for ever.' I'm told by Hebrew scholars that the verbs are very similar, and it might be either. You see which ever it might be it's awesome, because it may be God saying, 'Look, I'm going to take my spirit away from man. I'm going to leave him what he was when I made him man, just dust, nothing more. I'm going to take away that breath that I put in him.' Do you remember Paul's first chapter of the Epistle to the Romans? Time and time again he refers to man and says 'God gave them up.' He left them. And I sometimes marvel that He hasn't left us, with all our disobedience. If the meaning of the verb is 'strive', then it's not unlike what happened with Pharaoh, who kept on hardening his heart until last of all, it says, God heartened his heart. There comes a moment when He doesn't strive any more.

And the other side is,

*God's decision (verses 5 and 8).* Verse 5 is the other side to what we saw in our first study, when at the end of chapter 1 God saw in creation that everything was very good. Now in 6:5, 'Every imagination of the thoughts of his heart was only evil continually.'

Pause for a moment. This is a picture of the whole world full of wickedness, but it's also a picture of wickedness and death. The imagination – note the words – of the thoughts of the heart. So if you're going to change what people do out there, you've got to change what happens to people *in* there. What can we do about the violence in our society? There is no way law and order can stop it, not really ultimately. The only way we can do anything about it is to go deep into the hearts, the thoughts, of evil men and change them. Do you know, one of the plusses of our society is that humanism has been killed stone dead – that blissful hope that man was coming of age, that he was going to get better and better; all the evil things of the past would go. And we believed this to be the truth about man.

The miracle is that we don't have another judgement like the flood (but God says that until the final day there never will be another judgement like it). But will you notice that in verses 6 and 7 God says, 'I'm sorry I made man.' I once visited a mother whose child had gone so far astray that she said to me in tears, 'I'm almost sorry we ever had him.' I don't think I ever heard an indictment like that. And here's God, looking at the world He's made, and saying 'I'm sorry.' And I think I can say from the two strong verbs in verse 6, that God is involved, He cares, He's deeply involved in the world He's made. God suffers, and He judges only because He suffers. If you can easily sit in judgement it means you don't care very much. The more you believe in hell, the more sensitive you will be, because you care so deeply.

Sin grown. And before we move on, just notice that if God is going to judge man on a cosmic scale – there is that little phrase, 'Noah' (verse 8) 'found favour.' It's all the story of grace.

## Sin judged (chapters 6-11)

### The message of the flood
You may well know that there are many other records, besides the Old Testament, of a flood. You will find flood-myths and legends in many parts of the world. But they are very different from this. In the pagan accounts there are gods having a battle, or there are gods who can't sleep because man is making such a noise on earth so they send a flood to quieten him – but the biblical story of Noah is majestic, it's God-centred, it's relevant.

Note first of all that in verses 11 and 12 there's a picture of anarchy, corruption and violence. I think we still see it around. The Book of Judges says about those days, 'Every man did that which was right in his own eyes.' We're almost there in our society, and a society like that is poised for judgement. So it was then; and so comes the flood, a picture (because Jesus uses it) of universal judgement. Jesus said, 'As it was in the days of Noah, so will be the coming of the Son of Man.' What were they doing in the days of Noah? Well, they were doing evil things, but many more were just going round doing ordinary things; marrying, giving in marriage, carrying on their business; and then suddenly the flood, and its message, that God is a God of judgement.

You ask the question, was the flood over all the earth? Well, you can pursue this for a long time. 6:13, 17 and 7:4 talk of *all* flesh and *all* the earth, and I wouldn't object to those who believe it literally to be the whole world; but I don't think that that's the book's emphasis. It's talking about that part of the world that they knew, their world completely, utterly finished by the flood. The important thing to note, in 6:17, is that God brings it. 'I will bring a flood.' It wasn't some freak of nature; it wasn't a catastrophe that 'just happened'. It was God doing it.

This may seem hard to bear, but let me say it. If you don't believe that God is somewhere behind the catastrophes of our world you're in a very dangerous situation because you're believing the world has got out of His control. I don't believe that God sends disasters in the way that He sent the flood, but I do want to point out that you must wrestle with the fact that somewhere at least God allows them. He is sovereign and He's in control and He works through them. Once you drop that you've got far more problems than if you accept it and say 'I don't know why God does – but I know He does.'

And He sent the flood as His judgement. It was (7:10,11) like going back to before the creation, to the chaos there was before the Spirit moved and brought order into the world.

We'll be looking at the ark in our next study. But will you notice in verse 16, 'The Lord shut him in.' There was safety, security, peace; but you will know that as He shut him in, He shut all but a handful out. Nowhere can you get away from the solemnity that if you want to believe in heaven you must believe in hell; that if you want to believe that the Lord shuts his elect within the family of God, and that they're safe for all eternity, you are bound to believe that there are many who are shut out. In the parable of the ten virgins in Matthew 25:10, 'the door was shut'; and 2 Peter 3:6,7 tells us that this is a picture of the final judgement.

I believe that you and I should have a new concern for evangelism. They're outside! – and Jesus, using the story of Noah, says the day will come when we'll be divided; one shut in, the other out.

That's the message of the flood. (There's a lot more to it – there's no doubt about the historicity; the dating is very interesting, and it's not symbolic.) And the end of it came, and in chapter 9 they're out of the ark and they start again.

When they start again there's one difference. Is the same commission given to Noah as to Adam? Yes; but in verse 2, fear, dread, violence. And it's in that context that this interesting verse 6 comes: 'Whoever sheds the blood of man, by man shall his blood be shed; for God made man in His own image.' So God knows that sin will continue. He knows there must be some legislation. He is a God of justice.

Does that mean that every Christian should support capital punishment? Well, I don't think so, because there are other things in the Old Testament that call for capital punishment that we don't accept as needing capital punishment today – adultery, for instance. But I believe that this verse can be used to support a belief that capital punishment should be an ultimate sanction in certain circumstances. I respect Christians who disagree with me on that. But what I don't think you can disagree with is that this verse says that, because man is made in God's image, he deserves to be treated as man. It's not just wrong to take the life of a man who's in the image of God; he who does it is in the image of God and deserves to be punished as a responsible human being.

Well, it's a reminder. The flood is gone, and as we'll be seeing, there's a wonderful promise that there will never be a flood any more; but there will be a final judgement. There will be. The flood reminds us of it.

### The warning of Babel (chapter 11)

Chapter 11 really begins in 10:8, 9 with an intriguing man called Nimrod, who was the beginning of Babel. It suggests that he was a mighty man corrupted, like many mighty men, by power. Do you pray for people in positions of power? It's easy to criticise them – but do you pray for them? They are under special pressure.

It seems that Nimrod began to go wrong, and the Babel tower in chapter 11 was an awful mess. So let's listen to the warning of Babel. In the Bible, Babylon is used as a symbol of all that is opposed to God. Let's see why from these verses.

Verse 4: this is what they want to do. Here's humanism, here's man, made in the image of God but living without Him. The Book of Revelation says that the holy city will come down from God out of heaven; but they are trying to raise their own. Do you notice how prevalent today is the fist clenched and thrust into the face of God? And notice what they were doing it for. 'Let us make a name for ourselves lest we be scattered upon the face of the whole earth.' They were frightened. They wanted unity to keep themselves safe. Unity is not always God's will. Doesn't He want us all to be one? Not always; no. He sometimes wants to divide. You could argue that the church was at its weakest in history when it was absolutely one.

And here's the pathetic thing; verse 3, the stuff they built their tower of was very makeshift, and, verse 8, it was half-built. I wish I could hurl from the platform of the

Keswick Convention a word of defiance against those who imagine they can create a society apart from God! I want to say to many of our politicians and economists and sociologists, 'You've been leading people astray; you've been leading us to believe that we could somehow build a wonderful world of loving each other and living in peace – and look at the mess we're in!' And I want to say, that God may in these days be wanting to do with us what He did with Babel.

But just one qualification. God's judgement is absolutely fair (verse 5): 'The Lord came down to see.' He always acts in absolute, impartial judgement. Man proposes – that's the first four verses – and God disposes. He comes down in judgement, He divides, and instead of it being Babel (which means 'a city of God'), it becomes Baal, which means 'confusion'. People could no longer talk to each other.

But isn't it lovely that we don't live in Genesis any more? It's only the beginning; we've moved on. And isn't it wonderful that 2,000 years ago something happened which was the exact opposite of Babel? There was a day in the temple courts or in the upper room at Pentecost when the exact opposite happened; when everybody heard in their own tongues the wonderful works of God. We live on the other side of Pentecost. God who divided now unites; God has restored, He has brought man and woman together in a new bond which is not our unity but His, made by Him. 'At that time' (Zeph. 3:9) 'I will change the speech of the peoples to a pure speech, that all of them may call on the name of the Lord and served Him with one accord.' So we pray that God will tear down the tower of Babel and that He will build up His kingdom.

Did you know where the famous Hallelujah Chorus from Handel's *Messiah* comes in Scripture? From that point in Revelation where Babylon falls; when the great city that stands for opposition to God is destroyed. They

sing 'Hallelujah; for the Lord God omnipotent reigns.'
God will build His kingdom on the ruins of Babel. 'Where
sin increased, grace abounded all the more.' I hope we go
out solemnised about what is happening in the world and
our country, but not hopeless. Grace will triumph.

# 4. Salvation in God's World
# (Genesis 4-11)

For this last Bible study we are going to take yet another bird's-eye view of those same chapters we looked at yesterday. I'm glad we can end, not on the note of death, which was our theme then; nor on the note of sin, which was our theme the day before; but on the note of salvation in God's world. But of course, that can only be real because the other is real; take away the reality of sin and death and you automatically take away the reality of all we are going to enjoy today.

Our text is in a sense the New Testament text Romans 5:20: 'Where sin increased, grace abounded all the more.' It's not a balance, not a draw; not just grace and sin growing side by side. It is a victory. 'All the more grace abounded.' It's rather like Jesus saying, 'In the world tribulation; in me peace. But it's not a balance. Be of good cheer. I've won. I've overcome the world.' And I hope we shall leave here rejoicing in the victory of God's salvation.

We shall notice in these chapters how the truths of sin, death and salvation march side by side. After the fall, the promise of victory over Satan. After the flood, the great message of the remnant and the covenant, two great biblical words on which we will spend a little time today. And out of the ruins of Babel's tower, where yesterday we ended, the beginning of the story of the church. Of course these great truths are only seen in embryo in these chapters. But there is a special beauty in them when you see them in their beginnings. Oh, mercifully there is a lot more than that! You couldn't have much of a Keswick Convention if you only had Genesis 1-11 to go on. There is a lot more. But we are seeing it in embryo, like seeing a little baby born, all beautiful. It's got to grow up; it's got to develop; but we are seeing it at the beginning.

### God's offer

We will talk first of all about God's offer, for that's the Bible. And only then will we consider man's response. What about God's offer?

#### Victory over Satan

Glance back to 3:15. I only want to spend a minute or two on this because we studied it two days ago. We lightened it with a note of salvation; let's just glimpse it to round off the whole. There's the promise of victory where God says to the serpent, 'I'll put enmity between you and the woman, between your seed and her seed. He shall bruise your head. You shall bruise his heel.' We saw that as a picture of a coming Saviour; a reminder that one day, in another garden . . . for remember, the victory was won as much in Gethsemane as on the cross. By the time He goes to the cross He says, 'Not my will, but yours' – and He's ready. And there the seed of woman grappled with and gained victory over Satan (Colossians 2:15 tells you how). I reminded you that there is a remarkable fulfilment in Romans 16:20, 'The God of Peace will soon crush Satan under your feet.'

You know, the same principle applies. If we would experience the victory wrought by Jesus over Satan, in the garden and on the cross, then there will be a cost. Any church that's engaged in evangelism and lives in the light of God's victory knows there's always a price to pay. The Messiah, the One born of woman, had His heel bruised. It was costly to win our salvation; but it was complete.

One last thought. As Paul points out in Romans 5:12 onwards, and again in 1 Corinthians 15:22, 'As in Adam all die, so in Christ shall all be made alive.' What happened in the garden with Adam has been superseded in Christ. Because we are human, we are still in Adam. We are in Christ when we are redeemed. But Romans 5 goes on to remind us that all have sinned. It's not just in Adam God dealt with sin. In fact, it's every Adam – all of us have sinned. It's not just Adam's sin but yours and mine which has been gloriously superseded in Christ. 'In Adam all die, in Christ shall all be made alive.'

*The way back to God*
Genesis 3:15 is a promise, and we rejoice in it. Chapter 4 is what was already happening. Note verses 25 and 26; here's a people beginning to worship. Who told Cain and Abel to worship? It's almost as if man had within himself the sense of worship. And they had a sense of their unworthiness – they brought sacrifices. But, at the end of the chapter comes 'at that time men began to call on the name of the Lord.' Note two things about that phrase. One is the word 'the Lord, Jehovah'. I'm not going to get involved in the theologians' debates about the various names for God used in Genesis and their significance in terms of different narrative strands. But what I do know is that there *are* different names for God, and this is the great Jehovah covenant name, the name that becomes even more real (Exodus 3:13, 14) when God reveals Himself to Moses as 'I am that I am.' 'Men began to call upon the name of the Lord' – and that's one of the great definitions of worship.

Listen to this definition of the church in 1 Corinthians 1:2. 'To the church at Corinth, to those sanctified in Christ Jesus, called to be saints, together with all who in every

place call on the name of our Lord Jesus, their Lord and
ours.' And right from Genesis 4, right on through
1 Corinthians to Revelation, what we do as Christians is to
call Jesus 'Lord'.

One thought about that verse in 1 Corinthians – there's
real unity. I dared to say yesterday that there can be a unity
which is of the evil one and not of God, a monolithic
attempt to be one, which is thrust defiantly at God. There
are many ideas of unity around about which Christians will
be very unhappy. But here's the real unity – 'All who call
on the name of the Lord'. I'm happily one with them. I
never have any problem about the validity of people's
ministries. Some people spend hours discussing these
problems. I must be naive; I've not got the slightest
problem there. All who call Jesus 'Lord' and mean it, all
who worship in their different ways and call on Him as
Lord, are brothers and sisters in Christ. And here, if you
like, at the beginning, is the way back to worship. It comes
at the end of a chapter where Cain goes out from the
presence of the Lord (verse 16); but others began to go
back into the presence of the Lord, and, who knows? Cain
may have got there.

## Resurrection hope
Now to chapter 5. Yesterday we talked about those long
years of Methuselah and others, and I pointed out that
every one of them, however long they lived and whatever
the age may mean exactly, had the three words written
across their lives: 'and he died'. Now notice, there's one
little hope for the future. Not a big hope – that's coming
shortly. But a little hope. Jump on to 5:29. Lamech at 182
became the father of a son who would be called 'Noah',
and he began to look out with some hope. 'Out of the land
which the Lord has cursed, this one shall bring relief from
our work and the toil of our hands.' In the Bible lots of
prophecies hinge upon the birth of a child. Some of the
first prophecies in Scripture are by parents who are

rejoicing in the birth of children. And here's Lamech, longing that something might be different.

It's rather ironic, because in the days of Noah came the awful judgement of God. And I find this even more pathetic: around the world, in the midst of that monotonous repetition 'and he died', is a kind of hope that perhaps somewhere, sometime, something better will come. Lord Russell, who was a good man and cared about the world he lived in and built his whole philosophy on the assumption that man is basically good and can sort things out without any reference to God, wrote an autobiography of great despair. And what a great humanist says about life is this: 'Only triviality for a moment, and then nothing.'

I want to point out that here in verse 5 is not just a vain hope. Go back to verses 22-24 where there comes, alongside the monotonous repetition, a glorious anticipation. A brilliant star in the sky, Enoch, shines out. We know so little about him, don't we – but we know from verse 22 that 'he walked with God.' And again, notice that after the birth of Methuselah, that was perhaps the moment when something different happened in Enoch's life. 'He walked with God.' Genesis 6:9, 'Noah walked with God.' It becomes a great biblical theme of Christian living – walking with God. Remember it; the Christian life is basically a walk. It doesn't take much spirituality at a time like the Keswick Convention to mount up with wings like eagles. And every now and again we get a special task to do – like giving Bible readings at Keswick – and we run and are not weary. Ah, but the test of Philip Hacking's spirituality is not how he gives Bible readings at Keswick, but how he walks every day. That's the test. And the glory of the Christian faith is that we can walk with God.

Can I just throw out a little plea for the Old Testament? I hope these chapters have given you a new zeal for it. Don't think that the Old Testament is superseded by the New, and that there's nothing there that can help you in your Christian life. Think of the great people who have

walked with God. Abraham, a friend of God; Moses, who
saw Him face to face; Jacob, who wrestled with God. Oh,
these men knew their God! And they had so much less to
go on than we do.

And so what happens? He walks with God (verse 24)
'and he was not; for God took him.' Now, isn't that
lovely? You see even in the Old Testament there is a
reminder that death is not finally the victor. Even there,
just a glimpse of the resurrection, a glimpse that is enough
to prepare us for the glory of the New Testament.

He just kept on walking. And because he walked with
God, well, he just walked into eternity. Isn't that the
beginning of the resurrection hope? Paul said, 'Nothing
can separate us from the love of God in Jesus.' If you've
got a love relationship with Jesus that transcends time,
what does death do to that? Nothing. For the relationship
goes beyond the temporal, and you just go on walking.
Jesus said, when arguing with the Sadducees about the
resurrection, 'Don't forget: God says, I am the God of
Abraham, Isaac and Jacob.' Not 'I was'. He's not the God
of the dead, but the living. The resurrection hope. It's only
tiny, but sometimes 'small is beautiful'. Thank God, we
live on the other side of the fulfilment!

Now the two big offers of God, which begin here and
become great themes of Scripture. The remnant, and the
covenant.

*The remnant*
The remnant is the story of Noah, how the few (eight) were
saved and the thousands perished. 'Just the remnant'
becomes a great theme in Scripture. Do you know the
names of Isaiah's two sons? One was named Sheah-jashel.
What does 'Sheah-jashel' mean? 'A remnant shall return.'
Isaiah's children were given names that meant something.
He preached to his children. Yes, there will be judgement,
there will be disaster. But always, the few; and it's the
history of biblical revelation, and I believe it's a challenge

for today. God may yet do things in this country and in the world, through the remnant – the few who believe.

Now, what about this remnant? Of course, it's the story of Noah. We are in chapter 6. Notice, he is God's man, but please remember (6:8), it was all of grace. Noah was a good man (6:9), a blameless man. He walked with God. God chooses the right people. It is all of grace. He was a righteous man.

Would you also notice (verse 13) that God told Noah what He was going to do, as later He did with Abraham before the destruction of Sodom. Marvellous, to be a friend of God – but what a responsibility! God may be telling you that our nation is under judgement, and you may get the message and therefore believe it's your job to share it. But that won't be altogether popular. It wasn't in Noah's case. But, here was Noah. He was God's man.

Now what was God's method? It was that there should be salvation through judgement, like the Passover. The lamb had to be slain, judgement came, but God's people were brought out. There's nothing in the Bible to suggest that Christians won't have to suffer, nothing to suggest that we are immune from the problems of the world, but it suggests that *through* the suffering we shall come through triumphant. Now if we'd time, we could enjoy looking at the dimensions of the ark, and if you like mathematics, you can work out the shape of it and you can realise that it was quite some floating chest. There was nothing to guide it; it just – sort of – happened; and you were on the water, you were shut in by God (7:16), and you waited. In the ark were the animals. Interesting that some went in by sevens – they were needed for sacrifice.

But the *big* message of the ark is that God brought it, through deep waters, on to solid rock. Isn't that the gospel?

Just before I expand on that, can I point out to you, it all happened for Noah and his family because they made a response? 6:22, 'Noah did all that God commanded him.'

He had to obey – by faith, by obedience. And he went into that ark, into which nobody had ever been before, not knowing how it worked. And you and I can only enjoy the security of God's elect when we respond and get into that ark. 7:1-5, 'Go into that ark.' I guess most of us are safely inside. Oh, do remember, because we are in God's ark, we have got to learn to live together. Isn't it tragic how some Christians don't really get on with other people in the ark, and they sit in the far corner wondering why on earth God has bothered to preserve the others? 'I'm sure they ought not to be here . . . what a strange lot of elect we are!' But we are in the ark together. I guess we are all there? If not, I would get into that ark, if I were you. You need to get into that ark.

But I find an urgency in that Jesus takes up this passage in the Gospels, and says, 'As it was in the days of Noah, so will the coming of the Son of Man be.' Let us go out to others and say, 'Get in that ark.' It's the elect – but not the select.

'Through deep waters.' When you read the story you see that God will watch over His own in the midst of upheaval and bring them through. If you want to follow it through, read 1 Peter 3:18-21, in which Peter says that the people in the ark were saved through water, and goes on very daringly to say that baptism corresponds to this. Now I tread very delicately. May I point out, that you must never push the analogy too far? If you try then you are in the truest sense in deep water, for there were some in the story who were totally immersed and they are not the people we are talking about! They were left outside the ark. Peter is not talking about methods of baptism. What he is talking about is that our salvation is our being in Christ, and we have come through the waters into newness of life, and that is what baptism is all about, whatever the volume of water.

'Through deep waters.' Note the verse at the beginning of chapter 8, 'God remembered Noah.' I think that's

important; He will not forget us. You get the same verb in
19:29. God remembered. We must never take it for
granted. How do we know that because we are Christians
now we will be safe at the end of the day? How do we
know that we will not fall sō far from grace that we will be
thrown out of the ark? Ah, you see, God keeps His
promises. He is faithful and just to forgive us. He doesn't
forget. He watches over us, and through deep waters we
are brought on to solid rock.

And just quickly, in 8:15, 16, Noah is told after one year
and ten days to leave the ark. (Incidentally, it's not
symbolic or allegorical. It's just one year and ten days, it's
all terribly life-like. I'm always intrigued the way
commentators try to find some symbolism in the raven.
They are quite happy about the dove – that's full of
symbolism. But they are hard-pressed to find any
symbolism in the raven. Quite right; it was quite a simple
matter, you know. It was a fact of the story. No symbolism
at all. It's real, it's historical.) And now (8:15) God says,
'Go out; start afresh.' The exodus of Noah. Just one thing
about it. Note verse 20. What does He do first? He builds
an altar. Verse 21: God was pleased. 'And it was a sweet-
smelling savour.' You have come across that phrase
before: Ephesians 5:2. The sacrifice of Jesus on the cross
was a 'sweet-smelling savour'. This is a wonderful picture.
When God blesses you, when you come through deep
waters to the other side of some experience, do you
remember? It's easy to think of God *in* the storm. The
proof that you think it's real is if you remember Him *after*
the storm. Noah did.

And can I point out to you that there's a great promise
that comes after that sacrifice, and the promise is (verses
21 and 22) that God shall never judge the earth with a
flood any more. These verses are read every harvest-time in
almost every church in the country. If you lived in some
parts of India and Africa today, would you think God had
kept his promise? Ah, but surely what God is saying is that

there never will be this universal flood and there will always be provision; that if people began to care about each other then there wouldn't be need. Look at the story of Joseph; all the earth came and found provision. And look at the great theme in the New Testament of those who have, sharing with those who have not. God works, so often, through His people.

Well, there's the remnant, brought through deep waters on to solid rock.

And just one other offer of God, and it's the great word

*The covenant*
The covenant is a solemn promise, not a bargain. God doesn't bargain with sinful man; I am in no position to strike a bargain with almighty God. He offers, and He offers the covenant. Please note, the word comes first in Scripture in 6:18 and is then picked up again in chapter 9. I want to look at chapter 9 under two headings.

*God's provision for a sinful world.* When Noah and his family start all over again (note 9:1), it's the same commission as was given to Adam, 'Be fruitful and multiply' – there is a new world beginning. But it's not the same. We saw yesterday that there is the note of the need for capital punishment, at least at that point of time and possibly for ever. There is a reminder that there will always have to be sacrifice because there is always sin, and in verse 4 is the beginning of the great scarlet thread of Scripture – 'Without shedding of blood is no forgiveness.' Look on to Leviticus 17:11. Isn't it pathetic that it has become the key verse for Jehovah's Witnesses refusing blood transfusions? It's got nothing to do with that. What a mess you can make of Scripture if you want to be perverse. It's got everything to do with this tremendous thought that you cannot get to God without sacrifice, for blood speaks of the life – and remember, God gives the life. It's not a case of man preparing a sacrifice. It's God saying 'This is the sacrifice I want.' That's the note of propitiation in Scripture, God's provision for a sinful world.

*God's promise for a redeemed world.* God says to Noah (9:8) 'This is my covenant. I am going to establish it with you.' It's a universal covenant (verse 9) and an everlasting one (verse 16).

Right through Scripture, covenants always have an outward sign and a word of promise. This is the first. The second covenant was with Abraham, and the mark of it was circumcision; the third was with Moses, and the mark was the shedding of blood. The commandments were given as token of that covenant.

There is a word of promise, that He will never again destroy the earth. But there is always a symbol, a sacrament, an outward sign. The tragedy of Christian history, and I weigh my words carefully, is that some people get more excited about the sign than they do about the reality. And the tragic thing is that baptism, which is one of the signs of God's promise, and the communion service, a sign of God's promise, have become places of division and argument instead of glorious focal points of Christian unity. What is the mark here? Verse 13, it is the rainbow. Can't you imagine it? What a rainbow that must have been! And there is a lovely picture in verse 15: 'When I see it I will remember.' Oh, I do like that. God is so touching, so gracious. Do remember please, that in Revelation 4:3, there is a rainbow around the throne. 'In wrath, He remembers mercy.' When I stand before my Lord and Maker, He doesn't see me, He sees Christ. I am clothed in His righteousness alone. There is His covenant, and thank God, He keeps His covenant.

**Man's response**

*The seed of faith*

I think you all know that in Hebrews 11:1-7 you get the New Testament commentary on three of these characters who have been in our minds: Abel, Enoch and Noah. Each of them is an illustration of the response of faith. For one of the lovely little-things-in-embryo in Genesis 1-11 is the doctrine of justification by faith. I told you that next year is the 500th anniversary of the birth of Luther. He, like Wesley and many others, battled and sometimes suffered for – as well as being gloriously redeemed by – that doctrine. And it starts in Genesis 1-11. Why was Abel accepted? Because he gave his sacrifice in faith. Why was Enoch taken to be with God? Because by faith he walked. I don't think he saw God any more clearly than I do; possibly less clearly. But he walked by faith. And supremely, of course, Noah (Hebrews 11:7). Just think of that verse for a moment. Noah acted by faith. God said, 'Build an ark.' No sign; no flood. You just took God at His word. Nothing to go on. No Scripture, no church, probably no preacher. Just a word from God Himself. And Noah, because he believed, did what he was told. The first mark of the Christian life is obedience, when you take that step of sticking your neck out.

They must have satirised Noah. 'What a fool!' How often the work of faith is folly to the world. Building an ark? No sign of water! Taking God at His word. You fool!

Oh, no; 'You man of faith.'

But the faith of Noah was seen in works. You are saved by faith, but you are created unto good works. Anybody can say that they believe. No point in going from Keswick and telling people that you now have a tremendous faith. They'll say 'Show it!' And I hope you will.

It says in 2 Peter 2:5 that Noah was 'a preacher of righteousness'. Whether he literally preached we cannot be sure. But he preached, says Hebrews 11:7, by what he did. You preach sermons as much by the way you live as by what you say. And if in the midst of today's security-obsessed world you can learn to throw away money and give yourself in abandon to God – you are preaching! And the thing that Noah did was a message. He was like Ezekiel's watchman, and he was speaking to his generation. The seed of faith; it's all there, in embryo.

## The birth of the church

After the tower of Babel and God's judgement on sinful man comes the birth of the church. I have one preparatory thing to say. In Genesis 10 there are, experts tell me, seventy nations spoken of. That becomes for the Jew a symbol of the whole world. In those seventy nations, God chooses to work for the family of Shem – that's the end of Genesis 2. The family of Shem became the family of Abraham, or the Jewish people. I have actually come across people who want to proclaim that the descendants of Ham, the black peoples of Africa, are therefore inferior, because God chose to work through Shem. That is sheer, dangerous nonsense. For I tell you from the New Testament (Colossians 3:11) that in Christ Jesus, in the church, there is no more Jew and Gentile, no more Barbarian, Scythian, bond or free; Christ is all and in all. And wherever there is a church which wants to say that in the New Testament era one colour is superior to another, they deny the New Testament scripture. There is no such difference, and I hope that never from the Keswick platform goes anything that gives even the slightest glimmer of theat teaching. We're different – but superior? inferior? Never!

And you see it helps, because that is chapter 10; God planning His work through Abraham, and Abraham and his family are the precursors of the church. The church is born out of the ruins of Babel. Babel was man thrusting his own city to God; Abraham is the beginning of God bringing His city to man. That's the church.

But there's just a contrast, and quite an important one. It is today's world we are talking about. We are not living in the antiquarian past. It's what our world is like, what we are like. Note the contrast. In 11:27-32 is a story of

compromise. Terah, Abraham's father, sets out for
Canaan. (We know, from the New Testament, that
Abraham was called to go to the land of Canaan from the
civilised Ur of the Chaldees.) They go on a pilgrimage to
cross the river, to go across on the other side – the word
'Hebrew' may mean, 'those from the other side'. But
(verse 31) Terah settled in Haran.

If you want a contrast, compare 11:31 with 12:5.
'Abraham went to go into the land of Canaan; and into the
land of Canaan they came.' They went all the way. But
Terah? Settled half-way. I don't think I'm allegorising
Genesis 11 when I say that this is often the history of the
pseudo-church. Many who name the name of Christ and
call themselves churches compromise with the world. They
have made some step out of the world, but they are living
in compromise. They have gone half-way. And they do no
good to God and they do no good to the world. If Keswick
means anything, it is a call to come out and be different.

Not the naive idea of leaving your denomination and
joining a perfect church – they don't exist and never will.
Not that, but the challenge to be different, often in the
midst of the church to which you still belong. You may one
day think you cannot belong to it – but the important thing
is to stand out against the compromise that is the half-way
house of the pseudo-church.

And contrast the story of conquest. I just want to tell
you that when Abraham went out, says Hebrews 11:8-10,
not knowing where he was going, he went out by faith. He
kept going, he didn't settle half-way, he crossed over and
on he went, in the life of faith.

Now here, as I finish, is the church. In the strange plan of
God the church is called out of the church to go back into
the world. To change the world. It doesn't run away from
today's world, it doesn't try to pretent that all these issues
which we have in a sense skated over these past few days
are not real. It's a world of sin and death and judgement

and fear, and into that world we must go. We must seem to be part of that world – we can't help them if we live miles away in our own little cocoon – but we can't help them if we are not different spiritually. Nobody has bettered that simple and true phrase, 'in the world but not of the world'. It's to be like Jesus. And it will be my prayer that as Jesus, friend of publicans and sinners, lived in the world as salt and light, so we, His church, in the spirit of Abraham will go into today's world and be salt and light, preachers of righteousness, livers of faith, until this world becomes the kingdom of our God and His Christ. And He shall reign for ever and ever.

In the book of Daniel is a vision of a little stone that comes out of a mountain. There's the massive image of the world. And the stone topples over the image of the world, until it becomes a mountain which fills the whole world. We have been looking at the 'little stone'. But it did become that which, in the person of Jesus, toppled the image of the world. And one day, that glorious day when Christ returns, that stone will fill all things.

Meantime, God give us grace as we live in today's world, recreated in the image of God, redeemed by the second Adam, to go out to live to His praise and His glory; to snatch men from the waters and bring them into the ark; and to help God, who brings down His kingdom from on high, to help Him in the work of the kingdom; so that this world may again be His world, in the fullest sense.

# THE ADDRESSES

# 'WE WILL GIVE OURSELVES TO PRAYER, AND TO THE MINISTRY OF THE WORD'

*by Rev Eric Alexander*

## Acts 6:4

Many people have left Keswick after the week's convention, never to be the same again, because the living God has met with them and spoken to them. But we dare not presume that simply because we have come together God will automatically do the same for us this week. We need this evening in a special sense a fresh word from Him, and a fresh response from our own hearts so that we may come into His presence to hear what God would say to us. And I invite you to turn with me, for such a word from God, to the great apostolic resolve you will find in Acts 6:4. Let me say right away that my concern is that that resolve may be re-echoed in all our hearts as we set out into this convention together.

I think it is obvious in Acts that the establishing of these priorities so early in the church's life was absolutely crucial for its future. I have little doubt that a similar clarity in our approach to this convention could be quite crucial for its permanent profit in our lives and its significance for the cause of God more widely in the church and in our land. There is a significance, for the sake of the whole church, in our coming together like this, drawn, as we believe, by God's Spirit. And the establishing of this clarity in our whole approach to the convention is crucial.

I think you will recall the occasion when this became an issue for the early church. Of course establishing priorities is always a vital thing in every sphere; our time, energy and money are all limited, and we give away where our priorities really lie by the things to which we devote them. The apostles discovered that they had to clearly establish their priorities. It arose out of what almost seemed a trivial incident, but the principle that arises out of it is not incidental.

There was some ill-feeling, we read in the Revised Standard Version, between the Hellenists (Greek-speaking Jews) and the Hebrews (probably the Aramaic-speaking Jews); the Hellenists felt that their widows were being neglected in the distribution of food. It was a matter of social concern and practical Christian care for the needy.

Now the message of this passage is not that it is unimportant whether the church of Christ becomes a caring and concerned fellowship. That is a matter of enormous importance to God, and it ought to be so to us. But what is really important in the passage is what the apostles recognised. Here is a sinister attempt by Satan to divert them from the true business of their lives, and the whole future of the church was in a sense in the balance.

It had happened twice before. In Acts 4, the devil had sought to disable them through discouragement and opposition and persecution as Peter and John were imprisoned and commanded to speak no longer in the name of Jesus. They responded to that danger by coming into the presence of God and pleading with Him: 'Sovereign Lord!', they cried. In Acts 5, the whole issue is raised again of the sinister work of the devil in introducing hypocrisy into the church, and the incident of Ananias and Sapphira. That was the subtle intrusion of a diabolic attempt to disable or destroy the church of God.

Now in chapter 6 he seeks more subtly still, not only to come with division – though here was clearly the danger of murmuring, division, discord and disharmony and mutual suspicion; but the deeper danger was that the apostles might become absorbed with good things, and become distracted from the things that were vital. But they said, 'We will not be diverted; we will give ourselves to prayer and to the ministry of the Word.'

I believe that in the church of Jesus Christ in this generation we face precisely this kind of danger: that of forgetting where our true priorities lie, of failing to distinguish between the merely good, and the vital and fundamental. I believe there is nothing we need so much at this convention as a clarifying of our vision and a re-echoing of this holy determination of the apostles. The focus of our concentration needs to be here: 'We will give ourselves to prayer and to the ministry of the Word.'

Will you look with me, a little more closely, at these priorities. Firstly,

## We will give ourselves to prayer

The Authorised Version: 'We will give ourselves continually to prayer'. Phillips: '. . . whole-heartedly to prayer'. Another version: '. . . steadfastly in prayer'. What are they saying? Not simply that prayer is important, that every Christian ought to pray, every convention like this should begin the day with prayer, every church ought to have a prayer meeting; what they are saying is that the chief business of the church of Jesus Christ is prayer, and the greatest need of a confused and sick and desperately needy world is a praying church. Do we really believe that? One of the things that might make this convention a vast and eternal significance for our nation would be if we were to learn that what our nation needs in its confusion today, above everything else, is a praying church.

Let me spell this out a little more in two propositions which seem to me to arise from the context of this passage. You will notice, first of all, that I am not saying that 'prayer is the best way of supporting Christian work.'

What I am saying is that *prayer* is *the basic form of Christian work*. It is a consistent theme in Scripture: prayer is work. Paul cries out to the Romans – 'Strive together with me.' The word he uses is the word we have brought into our language as 'agony'. The real work which the apostles did was done in the place of prayer, and again and again it was this that brought down the power of God. And may I say to you that I am increasingly convinced that the reason we see so little of the power of God in the church of God today is that we have not discovered this principle, that the basic form of Christian work is prayer.

Professor O. Hallesby, in that remarkable little book *Prayer*, says that the work of prayer was a prerequisite for all other work in the kingdom for the simple reason that it is by prayer that we couple the powers of heaven to our helplessness. It is therefore necessary for the Spirit of God to burn this mystery into our hearts; that the most important work we have to do is that which must be done alone with God, away from the bustle of the world and the plaudits of men.

Let me add, the reason for this is quite simple. It is that *the work we are engaged in is not man's work but God's*. The only permanently significant things that will happen at Keswick will be those of God's doing, and therefore marvellous in our eyes. Do you really grasp that? There are many things man can do by himself. He can move people emotionally. He can convince them intellectually. He can indoctrinate them 'orthodoxly'. But only the living God can spiritually resurrect them, eternally save them, inwardly transform them into the image of the Lord Jesus; and this is what we are concerned with. It is God who gives the increase.

We are here in this week simply to wait upon God, that He would come down and touch our lives in some special way. We have known very little of true revival in this country in this century; but where it has happened, there is something! I have spoken to people who have known a little of it, in the Western Isles of Scotland. Something takes place which can never be mistaken merely for the accomplishments of men. We are here to wait upon God. And my plea to you is to keep your eyes upon Him, to set aside time really to wait upon Him.

Now there would be a corollary from these two propositions which would be very obvious to us (though eluding us in our practice); if this is God's work and not our own, then prayer would become fundamental rather than supplemental in our thinking about the service of God. That it is not, is the great tragedy of the Christian church.

Prayer is the basic form of Christian work. It is also the basic form of Christian warfare.

The apostolic church was clearly engaged, corporately and individually, in warfare. It was locked in mortal combat with the powers of darkness who resisted every advance of the kingdom of God; and that really is the record of the Acts, of advances by the church met by counter-thrusts from the powers of darkness coming in all sorts of ways. It happens individually as well as corporately. Let me say to you, that is the background in which we gather. Every move the Spirit of God makes in your life will be resisted by the powers of darkness. All true Christian living involves Christian warfare, and we need to be reminded that the pressures and difficulties that many of us are undergoing are 'par for the course' in Christian living.

But the real question we have to ask is, where is the front line? That is the fundamental question, where the issues are really being decided. Well, the biblical answer is clear. It is the place of prayer. That is the testimony of the whole book of Acts. The front line in every situation is to be found in the place of prayer.

Do you remember how it is illustrated supremely in Exodus 17? It was Israel's first battle after their release from Egypt, and the Amalekites came against them in Rephidim; and Moses the leader of God's people did a rather extraordinary thing; he left the battlefield, as it seemed. He said to Joshua: Choose men and go out and fight; as for me and those with me 'we will go to the mountain top.' And Moses and Aaron and Hur went to the mountain, and Joshua led the forces of God into battle, and the progress of the battle fluctuated astonishingly, until they recognised that the issue of the battle lay, not with the combatants on the field, but with the interceders on the mountain top. When Moses lifted up his hands Israel prevailed, and when he let them down Amalek did.

There are many people here from the overseas mission field; they have been battling, and please God that He may refresh them and restore them. But I want to say to you that the real place where the battle is fought for ministry such as theirs is in the place of prayer; and that is why Keswick may stand for something of immense significance for the work of God throughout the world, if we learn the lesson in these days and go from this place, saying 'We will give ourselves to prayer and to the ministry of the Word.'

There are various ways in which we can react to this apostolic determination. The commonest among evangelicals is to say, 'But there are other things that we need to do beside praying.' – 'Does the man not understand that we live in a complicated, confused world, with mountains of things to do besides praying? That's simplistic!' Well, there are other things we need to do. But that is not the lesson we need to learn. We are, by and large, good at these other things. This is the area where our Achilles heel is to be found; and maybe the most significant thing that could happen at Keswick would be for God to form and re-form our lives, personally and corporately, by this principle.

**We will give ourselves . . . to the ministry of the Word**

Now the other part of the apostles' resolve. It literally means, 'to the service of the Word'. It has the same root as 'to serve tables' in verse 2, and has precisely the same meaning. There was no distinction between these groups of people in terms of status; but the apostles had discovered this primary calling, that they were devoting themselves to be the servants of the Word of God. Now that implies two things; and it involves two things for us which I think are of crucial importance at the beginning of our convention.

First, it involves submission to the authority of God's Word. Now many of you might respond – 'it is to God that we are servants.' But you cannot be submitted to the one without being submitted to the authority of the other. Again and again through history this has been the focal point for the church, and it is so again today. I am sure that Francis Schaeffer is right when he speaks of this as the watershed for evangelicalism in our generation. This is where the crucial issues really concentrate for us, on our whole approach to Scripture, and perhaps above all our submission to its authority. Let me read you some words of Dr Packer: 'The decision facing Christians today is simply: will we take our lead at this point [that is, the point of authority of Scripture] from Jesus and the apostles, or not? Will we let ourselves be guided by a Bible received as inspired and therefore wholly true (for God is not the author of untruth), or will we strike out against our Lord and His most authoritative representatives, on a line of our own? If we do, we have already resolved in principle to be led not by the Bible as given, but by the Bible as we edit and reduce it . . .'[1]

My dear friends, there is something of vital importance for us here. God's honour and glory are involved in this whole issue. I pray that we may be a company of God's people bowed before God's book.

But the apostles' resolve involves something else; not only submitting to Scripture's authority, but preaching it as their ministry. They were not merely determining upon an academic attitude to Scripture. They not only served it – they served it up! That was the diet on which the early church grew and thrived, as Stephen witnessed to; what is it he goes out to do in this critical moment in the church's life? He goes out to proclaim holy Scripture in all its rich fullness.

Have you come hungry? I pray God that your hunger is for the bare Word of God, for that is all we are commissioned to declare. We have no 'Keswick blessing' dissociated from Scripture. God is always pleased to bless His people out of the words of Scripture, and we therefore come saying to Him that we will devote ourselves to the ministry of the Word. That means that we will call upon all the functions of our being, all our faculties, all our freshest intellectual and bodily powers, our whole affections – to be devoted to the Word of God, submitted to it, hungry for it.

We gather in crucial times; in many ways these are intriguing days. The Church has never more needed to have this holy resolve burned upon its soul: 'We will give ourselves to prayer, and to the ministry of the Word.' Will you say likewise, in covenant with God? Oh, may God be thus honoured, His Son exalted, and His people blessed, by such resolve.

1. Packer, J L *Understanding God's Word* (Lakeland, 1980), p.18

# 'WHAT DO YOU WANT?'

*by Dr Ronald Dunn*

## Mark 10:46-52

I was preaching in Dallas some time ago, and a woman who had been a member of one of my churches years ago came up afterwards. 'Well, Pastor,' she said, 'that was an old sermon you preached tonight!' I replied 'Yes, Madam, but your obedience will be brand new!' Most preaching consists of telling people what they already know but have not done anything about. So even though this passage in Mark 10 has been thoroughly used in Keswick year after year, I trust the Lord will make it fresh and new to us.

Some years ago I started a rather unusual collection. I collected foolish questions. They have always intrigued me, and how often we ask them! Someone sees you with your arm in a plaster-cast and asks 'Did you hurt your arm?' Someone sees you at the airport with all your bags packed. 'Oh, are you going on a trip?' Or you're just returning from a funeral. 'Where have you been?' asks someone. 'Ned's funeral,' you reply. 'Oh, is Ned dead?'

One of the first things that intrigued me about the story of Jesus and Bartimaeus was – without seeming to be irreverent – that it seems that the Lord asks a foolish question of this blind man. Bartimaeus, a beggar confined to a life of poverty and despair, sits beside the road and suddenly he hears that the Great Physician is passing by;

and immediately he begins crying out with a loud voice,
'Jesus, thou Son of David, have mercy on me!' Finally
Jesus stops, commands that the man be brought into His
presence, and asks him: 'What do you want me to do for
you?'

Well, I would think it's obvious; what else would a blind
man want from the Healer? It's like the question He asked
the man in John 5: a man, thirty-eight years a cripple, and
perhaps for thirty-eight years he's been beside that pool
waiting to get into the water because of the legend that
whoever got into the water after it had been troubled
would be healed; and perhaps for long years he'd been
there every day; and as He passes by, Jesus fixes His eyes
on that man and asks 'Would you like to be healed?' It's
almost as though He is mocking the man. What a foolish
question! Of *course* he wants to be healed! Why else is he
here? Why else, for thirty-eight years, has he been hoping
and praying?

But I have to remind myself, that the Lord never asks
foolish question, though they may seem foolish to us. He
never asks questions to gain information; He knew what
Bartimaeus was going to say before Bartimaeus knew it.
Nor does He ask questions like this to taunt us, to mock us
or humiliate us. He's not seeking information; but there's
a very real purpose behind His questions.

What must Bartimaeus have thought that day, when he
heard the news? Here was a man resigned to begging all his
life. There were no charitable organisations or
programmes in his day for someone like him. And that
road to Jericho was lined with beggars, hopeless and
helpless cases like himself. Perhaps one day some former
beggar friend, maybe, came by and said: 'Oh, Bartimaeus,
you should have been with me last week! I met that new
prophet from Nazareth, you know, Jesus, and guess what
He did, Bartimaeus? He healed me! I can see! Boy, you
should have been with me. I'll never have to beg again.
You *should* have been with me.' I'm sure he had heard

reports about the miraculous ministry that this strange preacher had.

And perhaps down in the depths of his heart he entertained the slight hope that maybe, one of these days . . . But those things happen to other people: those are the things you dream about. I think he was almost afraid that one day he would meet this Jesus.

Then one day he's sitting there begging. There's an unusual stir about. 'Jesus of Nazareth is passing by!' How his heart must have leaped within him – suddenly he doesn't know where He is because he can't see, and he just begins crying out: 'Jesus, thou Son of David, have pity on me!' Of course those around him are embarrassed, they try to quiet him down, but Bartimaeus' first chance is his only chance. So he cries out louder and louder, and finally Jesus stops and has him brought to Him; and He says 'What do you want me to do for you?'

I want to ask you, have you ever had a heartache? Have you ever been facing some problem? What would you have given to have Jesus suddenly appear in front of you and say 'What do you want me to do for you?' I tell you, there have been times in my life when I would have given everything I possess for Him to appear asking 'What do you want me to do for you?'

Can you think of any things? You see, I believe Jesus still passes by. I think in a very real sense He ministers to us. I don't think the Lord has changed. He came not to be ministered to, but to minister to. The reason He draws us together like this is not simply so that we may minister to Him but so that He may minister to us. We come this morning to worship Him, but more than that, He's come to minister to us and to meet us. I think it will transform this meeting, if you see yourselves as sitting in the presence of Jesus; and as our Lord moves up and down these aisles He stops before each one of us, and He asks 'What do you want me to do for you?' Is there anything you want Him to do for you (and my, what wouldn't you give to have Him do it)? I think as we stand on the threshold of another week of Convention, it would be good for us to centre on this question and on two others that I want to draw out of it.

### 'What do you want me to do for you?'

This, of course, is the first question. Maybe you have not even thought about it. Maybe like so many of us you've so got into the habit of going to meetings that you come without thinking, without giving any serious consideration to the possibility that something miraculous might happen to us. But if you leave this place today, and at the end of the week, the same person as you came, you've probably wasted your time. I believe that one of the results of meeting God is that we are changed. In one way, every time we meet the Lord there is a spiritual, eternal change wrought in our lives. And He's here, because we are here, and He's asking us the question 'What do you want me to do for you?'

Now why in the world would He ask that question, when He already knows the answer? I'd like to offer two suggestions. First of all, I think Jesus is probing us. He knew what the man would answer. But why ask? Anyone who has done any counselling knows that it sometimes takes a while to work around the surface issues. We're so afraid of exposing ourselves. We're so afraid that somebody will know our frailties that we send up a smoke screen. And many a time, the problem is in reaching behind the surface smoke to find out what the real issue is. I think the Lord has to deal with us this way.

### A probing question
The question in John 5 could be accurately translated: 'Do you really want to be healed? 'Oh, sure!' you say. You want to be, you act like you want to be, but is it what you

really want? I'm not so certain that we always know exactly what we want, unless we really think about it. Sometimes we answer too quickly the question, 'What do you want?' I think the Lord is probing these men. 'What do you really want?'

Here's this man; he's been a cripple for thirty-eight years.

'Do you really want to be healed?'

'Well, of course I want to be healed! . . . Well, I *suppose* I do.'

'Do you really want to be healed?'

'Well – I don't know – the more I get to thinking about it, I'm used to being an invalid, I'm so used to having people carry me wherever I go; I've never had to work, I've never had to take responsibility for my life . . . People don't expect things of me . . . You know, if I get healed, first thing is, people will expect me to get a job. If I want to go somewhere they won't carry me any longer. I'll have to start taking responsibility for my own life . . . I don't know about that . . .'

Do you know, it's true you can enjoy poor health? When you're sick everybody takes care of you, you get to watch what you want on television – it's nice; do we really want to be healed?

Do we really want revival? I know that everywhere people are praying for revival, but I'm not so certain we really want it. We say 'I want to be right with God' – but do we really? I think there are a lot of people in the churches who enjoy being in poor spiritual health. Do you know why? 'Well, the Lord never asks me to do too much because He knows I'm not well. The minister never asks me to do anything because he knows I'm not well. They never ask me to teach a Bible lesson. They don't expect me to give an offering. They don't expect me to come to prayer meetings or anything like that because . . . after all, I'm not *well*.'

Why, if I were to commit my life to Christ, if I were to

lay it all on the altar and come out one hundred percent for Christ – first thing you know, people would start expecting me to live like a Christian. I'd have to start acting like I were spiritually well!

I don't know whether we really want to be healed or not. So many of us have enjoyed the luxury of letting others carry the burden. Do we really want to meet God? I think He's probing us.

*A promising question*

I think there's something else even more important here. The very fact that Jesus asked the question is, I think, a promise that Jesus wants to do something. I don't believe He ever taunts us or mocks us, or plays cat and mouse with us.

Now I always like to say at least one profound thing in every sermon, and this is it, coming up. I believe, that my praying causes God to do some things that He otherwise would not do.

You say: I believe the Lord is sovereign. I do too; but I believe that within the sovereignty of God He has ordained that He works through the prayers of His people. I hear people say, 'Well I believe that what will be, will be.' I don't! 'Well, if it's God's will for me to have it, I'll have it.' I don't believe that! I think there are a lot of things that happen in this life that are not God's will. I know that there are some things that are predetermined and will happen regardless of what we do, but I believe that there are other things that God gives us a choice in, and He works through our faith and our availability and our willingness. I believe the Bible when it says that Jesus says: 'If you ask me I will do it.' And the implication is, that if you don't ask me, I won't do it. James said, 'Ye have not; why? Because ye ask not.' You may be surprised to discover that with only about three exceptions, Jesus never healed anybody until they asked Him first. As a matter of fact, on a number of occasions they had to practically run

Him down to get Him to heal them. And here Bartimaeus had to keep on yelling and yelling and yelling before Jesus ever stopped.

Has it ever bothered you that the Lord Jesus left more people sick than He left healed? If you'd had the power He had, wouldn't you have done wholesale healing? I'd have gone into every hospital, I'd have healed every sick person on the face of the earth. When I went to Bethany I wouldn't have said 'Lazarus, come forth'; I'd have said 'All of you come forth!' But the Lord, with only about three exceptions, never healed anybody until they asked Him.

Why is that? Well, I'm not sure. I think one reason is that the Lord wants us to admit our need, to admit that the problem is beyond our capability to handle or solve; and that's hard to do. It's going to put me in the place of total dependence upon Him. 'Without faith it is impossible to please Him,' and the greatest expression of my faith is my dependence upon the Lord. I'm confident that there are some things God wants to do for us this week, but He will not do it if we're too proud and stubborn to ask Him. I think the Lord is more anxious to heal us and meet our needs and give us revival than we are to receive it. But I know this: 'Ye have not, because ye ask not.'

It's a promising question.

## How badly do you want it?

This is Jesus' second question. How badly do you want it?

Have you ever listened to somebody play the piano magnificently and said to yourself, Oh, I'd give everything if I could play like that? You don't really mean that. If you meant it you'd be practising, working, disciplining yourself. What you really mean is, I wouldn't mind if the Lord gave me that ability – I wouldn't mind waking up in the morning with a talent like that. You see, most of us want these things, but not badly enough to pay the price.

'Bartimaeus, how badly do you want to be healed?'

First of all, he wanted it badly enough to ignore public opinion. Notice that Scripture says that they tried to hush him up. The implication in Luke's account is that even the disciples were trying to quieten him down. Can you imagine that? Here the Lord Jesus is passing by and He has His usual entourage that crowd about Him and suddenly there's a blind man causing an uproar; he's disturbing the worship service! They go over and try to quieten him down.

He started yelling. People said, 'Shush! Be quiet!' The more they tried to quiet him the louder he got. He didn't mind if he made a fool of himself. He wasn't concerned about what people thought. He wanted to get to Jesus and he wasn't going to let anything stop him. And I tell you there are many of us who refuse and fail to get what God has for us, because we're worried about what people may think.

Do you want it badly enough to get rid of any personal obstacles that might slow you down? Jesus called for him to come, 'and he, casting away his garment, sprang up and ran to Jesus.' The garment was the long outer flowing robe. You try running in that and you'll fall flat on your face.

I'll tell you what I have learned. Any time the Lord wants to do something for me, it always involves some act of obedience. He always asks me to come to Him; it invariably means throwing something aside. Usually there's some personal obstacle in my life that's slowing me down, hiding His face from me, hindering my progress. Are you willing to get rid of anything that hinders? You say, 'Oh, I want to meet the Lord!' May I say to you, I think we're as spiritual as we want to be. If I wanted to be closer to Him, I could be. If I wanted to be holier, I could be. If I wanted to be more devout, I could be. The problem isn't that God sets a limit. It's that I cling to things in my life that mean more to me than a deeper relationship with Jesus.

'He is a rewarder of those that diligently seek Him' – the Bible never promises a reward for those who search casually. 'Blessed are those that hunger and thirst after righteousness.' The Lord doesn't promise to bless a mild appetite. It's one starving for righteousness that He honours.

Do you want it badly enough? Are you wanting to say, 'Lord Jesus, whatever it takes to get to you this week, whatever in my life is slowing me down, whatever in my life is hindering me, I want what you have for me so badly this week that I'm willing to ignore public opinion. I'm willing to cast aside any personal obstacle: "Nothing between my soul and my Saviour, so that His blessed face may be seen".'

### 'What are you going to do with it when you get it?'

What do you want Jesus to do for you? How badly do you want it? and the last question is, What if the Lord were to heal you, or deliver you, or bless you? What if He were to give you what you're asking for? What would you do with it? You know, I'm sure that one reason the Lord withholds some blessings from us is that He knows what we would do with them. How easy it is to make promises! How many have said when sick, 'If the Lord heals me, I'll do this, and this . . .' and when God heals them they forget about the promises.

Let's watch what Bartimaeus does. Verse 51: 'Immediately he received his sight and followed Jesus in the way.' Watch, this is beautiful. Jesus cut him loose, gave him options. 'Go your way,' He said. And here's a man who's been blind possibly for his whole life; the thing he most coveted was eyesight. Now, suddenly, miracle of miracles, Jesus has given him what he longed for. What's the first thing he's going to do?

Well, he's been sitting on that road for years. Jericho was the Las Vegas of its day – the sin capital of the world.

And I suppose Bartimaeus had heard all the people coming down from Jericho talking about all they'd seen and done, and I imagine that he said, 'When I get my sight, first thing I'm going to do is go down to Jericho and see what it's all about.' But what is the first thing he does when he receives his sight? 'He followed Jesus in the way.'

Isn't that beautiful? 'I'm going to use this new eyesight you've given me, to glorify you.' I tell you what I believe; I believe that the Lord will give you anything that will make you a better disciple of Him.

What are you going to do with it? You may have come to this meeting with a broken heart. You may have come on the point of despair, saying, 'If God doesn't do something for me this week I don't know what I'll do.' Maybe your home is about to break up. Maybe you're a minister who's about to quit the ministry because of disappointment.

I believe the Lord wants to do something. I have no doubt but that He's called you here providentially, sovereignly, so that He may touch your eyes. But the question is, friend: what are you going to do with it? I'm convinced that one of our greatest sins is taking the blessing and gifts of God and using them selfishly without any thought of His glory. And I believe that the Lord Jesus stands ready and willing to give you whatever it takes to enable you to follow Him, and to make you His disciple.

What do you want Him to do for you?

# WORKING WITH THE SPIRIT WE HAVE

*by Rev Tom Houston*

## Romans 8:10

Talking about the Holy Spirit, and listening to other people talking about the Holy Spirit, is not the easiest thing in the world. Christians often get into a stew about Him in their experience; and would you go one stage further with me, and agree that there are preachers and others who exploit this situation in an unhealthy way? And yet, when we have grasped what this is all about, there is nothing more stabilising and more productive in us, than the knowledge that we have the Spirit of God. I want to assure you about that, and give you ways of thinking about it that will help you; and I have just three things to say.

### Be counting on the Spirit

The essential difference between a Christian in the New Testament sense and one who is not yet a Christian is that the one has the Spirit of God resident in his personality, and the other does not yet. We read in our chapter, 'If any man does not have the Spirit of Christ, he is none of His.' A man receives the Spirit of Christ in his life when he turns away from his sin and believes in Jesus Christ as Saviour and Lord. It happens right at the beginning of one's Christian life. And it's seen in two other pictures by which this essential difference and change is described in the New Testament.

It's described as being *born of the Spirit*. Nothing could be more eloquent than to say that the Spirit of God is the one by whom a new life comes, and it comes at the beginning. It's also described as being *baptised by the Spirit*. There are two main features of the picture of baptism. First is the note of initiation – it's a new start. Like circumcision, baptism was a rite of initiation to both Jews and pagans. To emphasise the inner nature of the change that made a man a Christian, John the Baptist, the evangelists and Paul all use the expression 'baptised by the Spirit'. And of course baptism has the sense of cleansing. 'He saved us,' says Paul, 'by the washing of regeneration and renewal by the Holy Spirit,' and in that verse you have 'born' of the Spirit and 'baptised' by the Spirit linked together. This, then, is the great fact we have to count on. All true Christians have received the Holy Spirit. All are born of one Spirit. As Paul says, 'By one Spirit we are baptised into one body,' and after Pentecost this is the great plus-factor in the lives of Christians. They have the Spirit. There's no hesitations, no doubts, no ifs and buts. The God 'with us' of the incarnation is real in our experience, in that the Spirit of God is now in us.

I want to draw your attention to something about the New Testament. The future tense of a verb does not occur in reference to the Holy Spirit in the lives of Christians later than Acts 2:38. Oh yes, the future tense is in the Old Testament: 'I will pour out my Spirit on all flesh,' says Joel. It's on the lips of John the Baptist: 'He will baptise you with the Holy Spirit.' Jesus uses it at the end of John's Gospel: 'I will pray the Father . . . He will give you another Counsellor . . .' Peter uses it for the last time on the day of Pentecost, when explaining what has happened: 'Repent and be baptised and you will receive the gift of the Holy Spirit.' After that, significantly, every reference to the Holy Spirit in the New Testament is in either the

present or the past tense. It *has* happened. He *has* come.
It's only in the future tense when it is linked in with past or
present, like 'He who sows to the Spirit will of the Spirit
reap eternal life.'

Romans has some of these great statements. 8:2 'The
law of the Spirit of life *has* set me free', 8:9 'You *are* in the
Spirit', 8:15 'You *have received* the Spirit', 8:23 'We *have*
the first-fruits of the Spirit', 8:26 'The Spirit *helps us*'.
And so in 1 Corinthians; ('We *have received* the Spirit
which is from God' . . . 'You *are* God's temple' . . . 'You
*were justified* in the Spirit of God' – and other references);
and in 2 Corinthians ('He *has given us* the Spirit . . .') and
in Galatians . . . and in Ephesians . . . and on to John.
Have I said enough? Does this sound like the future? No, it
sounds like now! So, at the beginning of our talk, I want
you to grasp this fact and count on it. If we are truly
Christ's we have the Spirit, we are born of the Spirit, we've
been baptised by the Spirit, as Paul says, and we need to
recognise this and count on it. We are not on our own.
God is at work in us, and we just need to ask Him to
control us and go on doing His work in us.

Ah, you may say, but that's all very well; but in my case,
or in the case of others, it certainly doesn't seem to be so!
Well, that brings me to my second point:

## Cramping the Spirit

Having the Spirit does not make the Christian life plain
sailing. The New Testament is quite clear about that. Do
you know where it says it most clearly? Later on in the
chapter we read earlier. Just listen with both ears! 'We
who have the first-fruits of the Spirit *groan* within
ourselves' (Romans 8:23). The way some people talk,
whenever you have the Spirit it's all light and joy, but
here's Paul saying that the mark of the Spirit can be an
inward groaning! Not a pleasant thing. And the New
Testament is quite clear; things can go wrong after we have

received the Holy Spirit, and it deals with the way these things can go wrong in a number of ways, one general and one particular. I want to go through these with you.

*In general* it states that after you become a Christian you have the option of either going the way of human nature or the way of the Spirit. Before, you don't have this option; afterwards, it becomes very real. Paul has four expressions to underline this choice. We can *walk* according to the flesh, or according to the Spirit. We can *live* according to the flesh, or according to the Spirit. We can have our minds *controlled* by the flesh or by the Spirit. And we can *sow* to the flesh or to the Spirit. You have an option. This is illustrated in Jesus; no sooner was He the recipient of the Holy Spirit at His baptism that He was driven by the same Spirit into the wilderness to be tested. Hunger, ostentation and dominance – the devil brought Him the things that very much come from the flesh, and He had immediately to choose whether He was going to yield and go the way of the flesh, or resist and continue following in the way of the Spirit. And we need to know that this is plain New Testament teaching; after we're Christians and after we have the Spirit, we have a choice of going His way, or going after the flesh.

There's an interesting story about one of the early Fathers, St Philip Neri. He was an irascible man who quarrelled easily. One day he felt he couldn't go on, and he ran to the chapel and begged Christ to free him of his anger. Then he walked out full of hope. As it happened the first person he met was one of the brothers who'd never aroused the slightest anger in him before, but now for the first time this brother was unpleasant to him. So Philip burst out in a rage. Then he went on and met another brother who had always been a source of comfort and consolation to him, and even this man answered him gruffly. So Philip ran back to the chapel and cast himself before the statue of Christ and said, 'Oh Lord, have I not asked to be free of this anger?' And the Lord answered, 'Yes, Philip, and for this reason I'm multiplying the occasions for you to learn!'

We will be given options by the Lord as to whether we're going to go the way of the Spirit or the way of the flesh. When the Spirit is given, a choice follows. And if we make the wrong choice it's as though there's a short-circuit in our experience, so the charge that was meant as energy for a purpose is dissipated and does nothing.

Now the *general* choice is made more *specific* by the use of four negative expressions in the New Testament, in our reaction to, and treatment of, the Holy Spirit.

The first is in the story of Ananias and Sapphira, in Acts 5. They sold their goods and tried to pretend that the part they brought to God was the whole. Peter's word to them was this. 'Why did you *lie* to the Holy Spirit?' Here the issue was dishonesty, before men and before God. In other words, it was a defect of character.

The second expression is in the story of Stephen, in Acts 7:51. The Jews were about to stone him. They had always resisted his message. He said, 'You always *resist* the Spirit.' This was their opposition to the truth, as you will see if you read the whole of chapter 7.

The third expression is in Ephesians 4:30, where it says we are not to grieve, or make sad, the Spirit of God, and if you examine the context there you'll find that it's in our relationships that he's bringing in that idea, that we can *grieve* the Holy Spirit.

And the fourth negative expression is in 1 Thessalonians 5:19, when he says '*Quench* not the Spirit,' and if you look at the context you'll find that it's in the context of the gifts of the Spirit and the service we render by means of these gifts.

So we have four negative expressions, and I believe that there is hardly any problem that Christians – that's you and me – have, in terms of ineffectiveness, weakness, dullness and defeat, that cannot be analysed and dealt with in terms of these or similar categories. When experience seems to contradict the great fact that we have the Spirit, for the believer it is not because he does not have the Spirit or is not baptised by the Spirit. It is because he is either lying to Him, resisting Him, grieving Him or quenching Him in some way and allowing the Spirit's power to drain away to no purpose because we are living according to the flesh. So, if your Christian experience is unsatisfactory and you are a Christian, then the need is to check yourself out at these points and rectify matters. To use the figure with which we began, we must cease cramping the Spirit's style.

But to see this rounded and whole it needs to be stated positively, and this brings me to my final point.

## Channelling the Spirit

In 1963 we visited Jordan, away back in those days before the six-day war. One of the things that impressed us was that we found a very different situation in Jordan in the South from Israel in the North. Though the climate, soil and rainfall were not very different, the results were different. In the South it was April; the wheat was about five inches high. When we got up near Galilee they were harvesting! And only a day or so in between. What was the difference? The difference was irrigation. There was a pipe in every field. The water was not only available, it was used. It was channelled to where it was needed.

Jesus likens the Spirit in the believer to rivers of living water. This, He says, will be given to those who believe in Him. Why is the result often poor? It's because that water is not brought to where it is needed. It runs away useless, as in the Jordan.

To take another illustration. I remember in 1968 we were in Ghana, and we were taken to visit President Nkrumah's great project, the Akosombo Dam; and as we went up and walked across it, and saw the sheets of water stretching back for miles behind the dam, we were impressed. And yet we'd come straight out of Accra and a country with a ruined economy! You could buy nothing in the shops. The students had wondered whether or not we could have a welcome meeting for the university mission, because there was no sugar. And yet there was a great dream, a dream of water and power, represented in that dam. Yet all around was a ruined economy. Why? Because Nkrumah didn't pay enough attention to the need to get the water and the power to where it would be productive. The water lines were poor, and Ghana had bad relationships with its neighbours by then, and part of the plan had been that they would buy water and now they wouldn't. So there was a great mass of water with tremendous power packed behind it – and a ruined economy.

Now I believe that many Christians have this approach to the Holy Spirit. They want power, they want mighty power; they take great steps to seek it – and yet it often comes to very little. Why? Because we have not known what the Holy Spirit is for, and how He may be brought to fulfil these purposes in our lives. Water is not always a blessing. I'm thinking of massive erosion in Tanzania; when the rain comes it comes in great storms; it goes charging down the hillsides carrying everything including soil with it. It leaves a totally barren area that you couldn't even drive over. The water is there; but because it was dissipated straight away it was destructive. It's only when it gets away from that area that it begins to be a blessing, and to be channelled into the crops that the people sow by the side of the river that they can control.

I believe that happens in the lives of believers. They allow experiences to charge through them like those stormy waters, and they express them in emotional ways, and they end up not much further forward; because what God has given has not been channelled for the purpose God has given it. I'm not saying anything about the nature of the experience, I'm speaking of its *purpose*. And I want to identify the four things for which the Spirit is given. You will find that they correspond to the four negatives of which we spoke earlier.

First, the Holy Spirit is given *to make our character like Jesus'*. Given to change our characters. He is a Spirit of Holiness, and He works in us the fruits of the Spirit, and it's in this respect we can lie to Him and prevent Him from working. Then, the Holy Spirit is given *to teach us*, so that we might have knowledge. He is the Spirit of truth and the thing He wants us to have is the truth; and it's there it's possible to resist Him.

Thirdly, the Holy Spirit is given *so that we may have good relationships*. He is the Spirit of love. 'The love of God is shed abroad in our hearts,' and it's here we may grieve Him, and what is affected, if we do, is unity. Finally, He is given to us *so that we may serve God*. He's the Spirit of power, and in relation to the gifts that He gives, we can serve Him. But if we're negative there then we quench the Spirit and the service is not given.

How do we get a pipe to each of these fields? How do we take and channel the Holy Spirit that we have already, into these four essential directions? Because that's where the problem is with us. It's not that the Holy Spirit is not there. It is that the irrigation system is not set up. Take the area of character. How does the Holy Spirit become channelled into a character like Jesus'? Well, it's by a definite pursuit of holiness. It starts with us discovering the sort of person we ought to be from the Word of God; examination of ourselves on a regular basis; repenting of sin and confessing that sin that hinders character development; and prayer that the Holy Spirit will make us like Him.

Do you have the means of doing that? Did you ever wonder why there are so many lists of sins in the Bible? Like in Mark 7, or 1 Corinthians 6, or Galatians 5, or the end of Romans 1? There's a different reason in every case, but I'll tell you a good thing to do. Use them as check lists and use one a week. Make self-examination a regular matter. That's how the pipe gets to the field of character. I don't know any other way, do you?

What about knowledge? He's the Spirit of truth. We want to grow in understanding – what's the pipe? You must know already – Bible study. So simple, isn't it! I would love to ask the question (but I'm not going to!), 'How many of you have read the whole Bible?' I know that in Bible Society meetings we clear the bookstalls of Bibles with plans for reading through the whole Bible, at the end. And I just have the suspicion that there are folk who have been Christians twenty, thirty, forty years, who've never read the whole Bible. How on earth they expect the Spirit of truth to do very much in their lives I don't know. Because the pipe that brings the Holy Spirit of truth ito the field of knowledge in our lives is the acquisition and keeping of understanding of this book.

And relationships – what is the pipe that brings the power of the Holy Spirit to our relationships at home, at work, with our friends, in our church and so on? Again it's not very difficult to understand. It is, working at active cultivation of harmonious relationships. Jesus implied that we would have trouble in this area, and He told us four things to do. He said 'Bless those who curse you.' Speak well of people. Then, 'Pray for those who despitefully use you.' Think positively about them before God. 'Do good,' is the third thing, and we've got to tackle it at the level of speech, and of thought, and of action. It's not going to happen just by hoping. You have to stop being negative! You have to start commending people, to look for the good instead of picking on the bad. You're never going to have the Holy Spirit get through to make good relationships until He's got that kind of pipe-system to work in. If you've shut off the pipe of well-speaking, of praying for your friends, of actually doing them good turns, you can't expect the Holy Spirit to get through and water that field of relationships. We need to pray

specifically for the people we meet and live and work with.
For we're stuck with them, and really they're gifts of God
to us, and the more difficult they are the bigger gift they
are!

And what about service? We need to discover and
develop our gifts. I have a very simple way of thinking
about the pipe that will bring the Holy Spirit to bear on the
service we render to Him.

When a person meets a need, and then meets it a second
time, he begins to say, 'This is something I can do!' When
they've done it ten times they begin to think 'This is a gift I
have!' When other people recognise that the gift is being
exercised, they see it as a role and sometimes it goes
further. Then it's converted into an 'office', a job given
you officially. That's the secret: a need matched by a
response, that reveals a gift, repeated becomes a service,
kept up becomes a role; sometimes in the church, even at
work, they'll acknowledge it by giving you authority of
office. And the pipe in that little complex is 'Try it and
see.'

The whole question of the gifts of the Spirit has too many
clouds over it. If you will just try out this and that, and
work out where God is blessing you and others recognise
that you're good at it, then the gift will come, and the
church will affirm it. So what I'm saying to you and to
myself again is this; set up these pipes and you'll soon
know that the Spirit is flowing in your area of character, of
knowledge, of relationships and of service.

And oh, the great need is for maintenance. If we're to
know the Holy Spirit in our lives it calls for daily, weekly,
regular maintenance. Yes, there's a daily servicing, and a
weekly, and a monthly, and maybe a half-yearly servicing
we all need in this area. We need to plan time for that, and
then we'll know the Spirit flowing and flowing well.

In conclusion: there's a sin which the spiritual Fathers of
the East called 'spiritual greed'. It consists of wanting to

have more and more of God, unrelated to the specific
needs of your life and service. May God deliver us from
this vague lust for power, and help us set up the pipe-lines
that will enable us to work with the Spirit we already have.

# 'ALL AT ONCE AN ANGEL TOUCHED HIM . . .'

*by Rev Harry Kilbride*

## 1 Kings 19:1-9

I am sure you will have realised, if you didn't know this passage already, that Elijah is in a very bad way. It's hard to believe that this great and brave prophet could get so spiritually low as he did when he sank down in the desert under a broom tree or juniper tree.

I doubt if there has been a braver prophet of the Lord than Elijah. This is Elijah who stood before Ahab, who confronted the prophets of Baal on Mount Carmel, who challenged Jezebel; this is Elijah who prayed earnestly, and God heard his prayer for the withholding of rain and the giving of fire. This is Elijah who, later on, was to meet with the Lord Jesus Christ in a mysterious, miraculous, wonderful appearance when the Lord met with Moses and Elijah. Elijah – one of the greatest men of faith in the Bible. A man of faith, courage, prayer, faithfulness in the Lord's service. And yet here he is in this famous story, so depressed, so low, that he's even suicidal. 'I've had enough, Lord. I just can't go on any longer. I'm finished! Take my life away! I want to die.'

I feel a burden on my heart that I may be speaking in God's name to perhaps just one person; you may not be as low as Elijah was, but nevertheless you feel that you've just had enough. You may feel you've had enough of the ministry you've been doing; you may be a pastor or a minister of the gospel; you may be an evangelist, or a Christian worker – and you feel you've had enough. You're disappointed and disillusioned. Something or someone has let you down – in fact, if the truth be known, you feel God has let you down. Whatever it is – maybe something in your home, it may be because of your husband or your wife or some other circumstance – you have come to Keswick feeling that you can't go on. You may not have got to the point of wishing that God would take you to heaven, but nevertheless you feel much like Elijah. Or there may be somebody else who feels like that, and you want to reach out and help them. I pray that in the 'touch of the angel', as we consider it, there may come the touch of the Lord Himself to your heart, or, through you, to another heart. Here was Elijah, in this terrible state; and all at once, an angel touched him.

## It was a gracious touch

Let's consider what God did *not* do. God could have touched him with the rod of correction and punished him. After all that God had done for Elijah – providing for him wonderfully at the brook Kerith, and then through the widow of Zarephath, providing for him all those years; and protecting him from the wrath of Jezebel and answering his prayers with supernatural demonstrations of power – it's rather sad to see Elijah now self-pitying, however much we feel sympathy and empathy for him. If you go on with the story you'll even find a little self-righteousness and anger with God. And so God could justly have dealt with him otherwise than He did. He could have ignored him; dismissed him, without notice, without a pension, and said 'If that's how you are I'm finished with you as one of my servants. You've forfeited your job.' He could have sent an angel to condemn him, give him a message of God's anger. He could have killed him – that was what he had demanded.

He didn't do any of those things. The Psalmist says that

the Lord does not deal with us as our sins deserve. He is a gracious God. 'All at once an angel touched him' – and it was not a wrathful, punishing touch, not a touch that he deserved, but a gracious touch.

## It was a caring touch

I believe that this was a caring, gentle, loving, reassuring touch. Have you ever had anybody touch you like that at a significant moment? Just the touch told you that they cared, that they would do anything they could to help your need.

When we were first married we were schoolteachers, and my wife, who was working as a teacher as well as looking after me and the household, got very tired indeed. I remember the doctor telling me, 'Just make sure she gets plenty of T.L.C.' Do you know what that means? Tender loving care! Do you know, we have a God who gives His children tender, loving care? The writer to the Hebrews says (1:14) 'Angels are ministering spirits sent to *care for* God's elect.' You see, 'The Lord knoweth our frame; He remembers that we are as dust.' As we were learning in the Bible reading this morning[1], we're made in the image and likeness of God, yet we're not gods, we're frail children of dust.

How did Elijah come to be in this condition? God knew. For one thing, he was afraid. Look at verse 3, and verse 10. 'Now they are trying to kill me.' Everybody's against me! Jezebel has got notices posted on every tree – 'WANTED – dead or alive – Elijah!'

He ran for his life. He felt afraid, depressed, deserted; a failure (verse 4). 'I am no better than my ancestors . . . my ministry's failed; I hoped for a great revival. I thought Jezebel would be finished and all Baal-worship banished for ever. It was short-lived. I'm finished. I've had enough, Lord. I'm going to give up.'

He was depressed all right, and he wasn't the only one of

God's servants in the Bible to be so. Job cursed the day of his birth. Look at Jeremiah 20:14; Jeremiah also cursed the day *he* was born. He feels so bad. And David – 'My tears have been my food day and night, while men say to me, "Where is your God?" '

He was irrational. When we get low we tend to say silly things. Elijah was running for his life because he was afraid that Jezebel was going to kill him. He says to God, 'Take away my life.' God could have said, 'Well, if you'd stayed in Samaria we could have taken care of that . . .' You see, Elijah was all mixed up. He had lost his faith (I don't mean his *saving* faith, I don't believe you can ever lose that; but he had lost his *experimental* faith, his daily trust in God). 'I've had enough of the battle, I've had enough of the ministry, I've had enough of threats . . .' But 'all at once, an angel touched him.' So gentle the touch, so caring the word; 'The journey is too much for you.' Not only the journey to Horeb, but the journey through life, serving your Lord.

### It was a practical touch

Did you notice how practical this touch was? No sermon from the messenger. The angel gave him sleep. You see he was very tired. He needed sleep, his body was exhausted. If you know the story of Elijah you'll know all he'd been doing recently – for one thing, he'd been busy praying, and that's hard work, especially earnest, effectual prayer. And he'd been executing the prophets of Baal in the name of the Lord; he'd run eighteen miles before Ahab's chariot; and though he did it in the Spirit of God, I believe that it took its toll on his body. He needed to rest; instead of that, he journeyed ninety miles south to Beersheba, left his servant there and then unwisely went another twenty or so miles further into the desert. In the burning heat of the day this tired man journeyed on.

He needed sleep, and the angel gave him sleep. He

needed food and drink, and the angel gave him food and drink. Have you ever considered that when you get low, there might be a physical reason for it? Sometimes we try to do too much, we don't take enough rest. Sometimes we don't heed the wise words that were brought to our attention this morning[2], that it was God's creation ordinance that we should have one day's rest in seven. I used to be impressed by a phrase used about Christian work – 'I'd rather wear out than rust out.' Sounds good, doesn't it? Then I read in a book by Francis Dixon, 'Yes – but what if the Lord wants you to *last* out?' That was a word from the Lord to me, not that we should become lazy, but that we should look after this body. We get tired, we get exhausted, we suffer pressure and sometimes we suffer reaction. Without going into the psychology of it, I think Elijah had a great 'high' on Mount Carmel. But now that it wasn't working out the way he thought it would, and Jezebel was still alive and kicking, he went right down low.

So it can sometimes be with us, and we just need some practical things – a holiday, a rest – to get away from it all and to be refreshed in body and mind and spirit.

### It was a personal touch

A touch is something personal, isn't it? There was a human form there, a person; a ministering spirit, but real, solid. So often we have the idea that whenever an angel appears to somebody they have great wings and shining lights and everything. When I read my Bible I think that that was a rare thing rather than the norm. So often these visitors appear in ordinary human form, as when Abraham entertained three strangers. He was unaware that they were angels. And I believe that one of them was a theophany of the Lord Jesus Christ. He appeared to him! And here was God, in His gracious, caring love for His prophet, giving him what he needed because he'd left his servant behind at

Beersheba. He needed a personal touch – and there was somebody there! You see marks of human activity. There was food, and a fire. I mean – God could have done all that by a word; He didn't have to send an angel; but He did that because He wanted Elijah to have the personal touch – and so He provided for his food.

Many of us thank God for the people who have given us the personal touch. I remember once I was in hospital with something which was diagnosed as 'acute pancreatitis' – I didn't know what it was, I'd never heard of my pancreas. The only cure was evidently to put a tube up my nose and down into my stomach to drain everything for a week, and also to feed me intravenously. I dreaded mornings and evenings because penicillin injections in my leg had been prescribed. Furthermore I couldn't sleep, and I was lying awake night after night, and by the end of the week I hadn't got a radiant testimony at all. I was really low. I think my favourite passage would have been 1 Kings chapter 19.

In the middle of one night a nurse came to adjust the drip, saw my eyes open, and said, 'Can't you sleep?' 'No,' I said – very self-pityingly – 'I never can sleep.' Usually they said they were very sorry that they couldn't give me a sleeping pill (you couldn't get it down the tube . . .) but instead of saying that, she asked me where my church was. I told her. Suddenly I said, 'Are you a Christian?' 'Yes,' she said. 'Oh!' I cried, 'Sit down and talk to me!' I just wanted to hug her, but it's very difficult when you're full of tubes, and anyway Kingston General Hospital doesn't allow the patients to hug the nurses!

She talked to me through the night whenever she came by. Do you know, my attitude changed. I could have said to her, 'You're like an angel of the Lord to me.' I think I probably did.

'All at once, an angel touched him.' Could you be an angel to somebody like that? Let God give us eyes of compassion, to see people who are low, people who for some reason or other have got right down. Maybe they're self-righteous, self-pitying – but there may come a time when we're like that; and oh, how lovely it is when someone comes. Maybe they say very little, just give us something, squeeze the arm, touch the hand – and you know someone cares.

## It was a purposeful touch

I must end with this; you see, God had further things for Elijah to do. He wasn't going to let him die, because he had some further ministry. This touch from the angel was to help him on his journey to Horeb, to Mount Sinai, where God was going to give him his new commission and meet with him.

'I've come to the end!' says Elijah. 'No, you haven't,' says God. 'I'm *finished*!' – 'No, you're not,' says God. 'Come, I have a date to meet you – at Horeb . . . at Sinai . . . (at Keswick?) . . . Come aside, come away from the things that have brought you low, because I want to meet with you.'

It's a message in itself, of course, what happened at Horeb. Read it for yourself – fascinating! Elijah was given a new vision, a new manifestation of the greatness and power of God. I believe, dear brother and sister, that when we get low, when we get under the juniper tree, we do need the tenderness of God; and sometimes we need to see again His greatness. And then we realise how silly we've been to be the way we are, for we serve a great God who can do anything. Jezebel? Who's Jezebel, before the throne of the Lord God Omnipotent who reigns!

But God also whispered his name, for He didn't speak to him in the noise; He spoke to him in the stillness, in the quietness, and He whispered his name. 'What are you doing here, Elijah?' Elijah was honest before God – there was no point in being anything else! So he told God how it was and the way he felt. And then God told him, 'Things are not what they seem. You think you're the only one left, do you? Are you omniscient? I've got 7,000 who haven't bowed the knee to Baal. You don't know who they are. That's my business, not yours. You get on and do what I want you to do.' Then He gave him a re-commission. 'Go back the way you came' (19:15).

'All at once an angel touched him' – and lifted him up to meet with God, and God said, 'Go back.' I believe with all my heart, that this is God's message for somebody here. He does love you, He does care for you. He's not punishing you. But He wants you to go back, and serve Him afresh. May God help you and me to do it, for His name's sake.

1. Philip Hacking's Bible readings in the present volume, p.65
2. Ibid., p.74

# THE RESTORER OF LOST YEARS

*by Rev Gilbert Kirby*

*This address was given immediately after that by Harry Kilbride which precedes it in this volume.*

## Hosea 1-14

I'm going to ask you to find Hosea in your Bibles. I wish, by the way, that we didn't call these prophets the 'Minor Prophets' – it does them an injustice, because I feel that God is speaking to us today as a nation and a church through these prophets of old. They are so relevant! Perhaps more so, in a sense, than any other passages of the Old Testament.

Hosea preached against a background incredibly similar to ours. It was one of the darkest periods in Israel's history. You know, it's lovely being at Keswick, and on a fine day it's absolutely glorious. But – dare I say it? – it's almost unreal. Because it's so beautiful we tend to forget what the rest of the world is like. Well, I believe it's good to do that sometimes; Jesus went up into the mountain; but tonight I've got to remind you of the world from which you have come and to which shortly you will return.

Hosea's personal life was a tragedy. His marriage was a tragedy. He was married to a woman called Gomer, who bore him three children; but she was unfaithful, left him, and became a prostitute. And yet God said to Hosea, 'Seek her out, buy her back and receive her again as your wife.' That was a pretty tough thing for any man to do. But this was a reflection of God's grace towards His people. Israel proved unfaithful and this was a way of illustrating it to the people, the way the prophet showed love to an unfaithful wife. If you want to know what the land was like at that time, a few verses here and there will show us. Hosea 4:1-3: 'There is no faithfulness, no love, no acknowledgement of God in the land . . .' Idolatry had taken over, as it says later in that chapter: 'Ephraim is joined to idols.' Yet the people seemed unrepentant and God for a time seemed to depart from them and leave them to their own devices (5:14, 15).

God still yearned over them; they were still His people; He still loved them; but they didn't love Him. He longed to bless them but they still persisted in their wicked ways (7:1-2). And the real tragedy of the whole thing was that as a nation they didn't seem to realise the state they were in. They seemed blissfully ignorant of their real condition.

And so I come to the verse which is the core of what I want to say: it's chapter 7 verse 9. 'Foreigners sap his strength, but he does not realise it. His hair is sprinkled with grey, but he does not notice.' Are we grey? Some of us have, physically speaking, passed that way some time ago. Some of us have passed beyond it and lost our hair altogether! But are we going grey in a wider sense? You see — I hate to say it, for I'm saying it to so many of my own age group here — going grey is a sign of decadence. You are not what you were. You used to have a fine head of auburn, brunette or whatever; now you are going grey, and it's a sign that you are not what you were.

Are we going grey? For example, as a nation? Whatever we like to say we've had a reputation in the world for generations, in all sorts of ways. But are we going grey, allowing our standards to be whittled away? Are we rejecting the absolutes that once we recognised? Are we condoning things we should be condemning? Is it happening subtly, slowly, without our realising it?

Think first of the moral aspect. Think of sex and marriage, the subjects so often mentioned today. Even in some Christian circles – as Philip mentioned this morning[1] – are we going grey, countenancing some things we should be condemning? Have we forgotten that marriage is a divine ordinance and a life-long institution? Are we adopting lowered standards or condoning them? Take the matter of homosexuality. I feel deeply for people who have problems in this area. They need compassion, they need help, expert help; but how can we, in the light of Scripture, condone homosexual practices? How can we possibly say God doesn't care about them? Take the question of the sanctity of life, God's gift to us. In Him we live and move and have our being – and yet we are prepared to let people have abortions, and unborn children are murdered – for that's what it is – for social convenience. Oh, there may be cases, I recognise that, when abortion could be possibly legalised, but never for the wide range of reasons that obtain today. London is becoming the abortion centre of the world. Take euthanasia – there's a great demand today for people to be allowed to end their lives, for doctors to be allowed to hasten the end; but life is not at our disposal. How, from a Christian viewpoint, can we possibly condone any legislation that's envisaged along these lines? – and yet we're so tolerant, so easy-going.

And some Christians are going grey in the area of materialism too. We follow someone who said, 'If any man will come after me, let him deny himself and take up his cross daily and follow me.' And yet, to look around at the Christian scene tody, many many Christians are just as materialistic as their non-Christian neighbours. They want every thing, every luxury, that everybody else has.

Not only morally but doctrinally also. It's a good many years since *Honest to God* was published. It caused quite a stir at the time, but there has been a lot published since. More recently there was *The Myth of God Incarnate*, published by some learned clerics. Doubt was cast on the incarnation; the sinlessness of Christ was questioned; the miracles explained away; the atoning death of Crhist has often been denied; the real resurrection of Christ, His ascension, His coming again, the doctrine of the Trinity – all these essential Christian doctrines have been questioned, even by religious leaders.

I ask you, are we going grey spiritually? In our churches – evangelical, Bible-believing Christians? Now, you say, we are nothing to do with the lot you have been describing, we can sign any doctrinal basis you put before us, we're not going grey – we're as sound as ever we were. In some cases, it's a question of being sound asleep. Are we going grey in the area of prayer and prayerlessness? Oh, we pay a lot of lip service, we write books galore on the subject, we preach, we talk about it, we discuss it; but when you look at the story of many of our evangelical churches and you look at their prayer life, you're bound to say, we're going grey. We may not realise it, but if prayer is anything to go by, we are.

Are we going grey in the matter of consecration? How many people are there in our churches who will say, if there's a regular need for a job to be done like teaching in the Sunday School or a Bible class, 'No, don't count on me every week, but if you're really in a hole, I'll help.' I've heard it so many times. In the matter of character, sheer Christian character – are we going grey? Aren't some of us very far from what we ought to be? Proud, perhaps; jealous, envious, discontented, fractious, touchy . . . are we going grey?

Now what happens when you're going grey? What do you do? Why, you dye your hair of course, don't you. And we do use verbal cosmetics. On moral issues we say, 'Oh, well, the world's very different today. You can't draw the line like you used to . . . You can't say this is right and that is wrong like you used to . . .' The polite word for that is 'situation ethics'. It means you compromise at every turn. It's a verbal cosmetic to cover our grey hairs.

When it comes to doctrine, we say that we live in a scientific and technological age. 'We can't believe in miracles like they used to; they didn't know any different.' 'We must re-interpret the Scriptures in the light of the age in which we live.' 'If we want to reach people it's no good talking about these miracles as though they were historical facts.' Another piece of verbal cosmetic.

When it comes to spiritual issues: 'Oh, yes, I know I'm bad-tempered and don't pray as much as I should, and I know this and I know that but you see the pressures of life are so much greater today, it's a different sort of life and you've got to make allowances.' Are we excusing ourselves? Going grey? Why do we do this? How is it we won't face these things?

May I suggest three reasons why we could be going grey without realising it.

1. *We haven't looked in the mirror lately*. Now, if I asked everybody here when they last looked in a mirror, everybody would say, 'Well, I've done it at least three times today.' Yes; but have you looked in the mirror of God's Word lately? Have you measured yourself against God's standard recently? Because when you do, you may discover that you're going grey.

2. *We don't like facing reality*. We like to live in a sort of cloud-cuckoo land. We don't like scratching beneath the veneer and revealing what's really underneath. We run away from being real people.

3. *We're not open enough with one another*. The last thing I would want to propose is that we go round picking holes in one another. Anybody can do that. But if you really love people and you've got a right relationship with them, surely there are times when you can help them if you notice they are slipping. I mean it might not be very tactful to go up to somebody, particularly if they are fairly young, and say 'I wonder if you've noticed; you have a few grey hairs

coming.' I don't think you would be awfully popular! You might possibly do it if the relationship is a very real, loving one. But what's far more important is that if someone you really care about is slipping and they don't realise it, if they're getting farther away from God, and if with a gentle touch and a loving touch and a caring touch you could help them recognise what's happening to them, and help them get right with God – you would do it.

You see we are going grey as a nation. The church, sadly, has been going grey for a long time. It may be that some of us as individuals have been going grey and we haven't realised it. It may be that God has brought us here in order that we might look into the mirror and say: 'God is right, I am going grey and it's time I faced up to it. I'm not the person I was.' How often we say that from a physical point of view! I don't think I could climb Skiddaw mountain today. I haven't enough breath. Well, it's nothing to be ashamed of. There are compensations in growing old.

But spiritually, it's another story. There's no need to grow old spiritually. Though our outward man perish, inwardly we can be renewed day by day . . .

But if we're going to put matters right, we've got to be real with ourselves and with God and we've got to face up to the people we really are.

We've been looking at Hosea. But there's another minor prophet with much the same sort of message. Joel spoke to the nation in much the same way as Hosea did. And he put things a little differently and he said as from God to the people, 'I will restore to you the years that the locusts have eaten.' I love that phrase. The wasted years. 'I'll bring back to you what you've been missing all these years.' Just as God says through Hosea: 'I'll bring back that youthfulness, that loveliness, that dynamic Christian living you once knew. You've been going grey.' Those grey hairs can be removed. But do face the fact that they're there; do look in the mirror and see if you've been going grey.

I imagine that in a convention like this, nearly everybody has committed their life to Christ. But you know committed Christians have to have various times in their lives when they face up to where they really are at that point. And I believe that God wants us before we go to sleep tonight to look into the mirror and see whether or not we're going grey.

Going grey is almost always gradual and imperceptible. There are a few who deliberately turn their back on all they've stood for, and walk out, as it were, and say 'I'm finished.' That's terrible; that's apostasy. We're not guilty of that; you'd have walked out by now if you had, or else you wouldn't have been here in the first place. Going grey is usually gradual. Little by little, things fall away; little by little, you drop doing the things you once did; little by little you become less keen, less committed, less concerned about the will of God. Brother; sister; beloved in the Lord. If you're going grey it's got to stop. It doesn't matter physically if you've grey hair or no hairs at all, but it does matter spiritually, it matters enormously.

Are you going grey? Are you missing out? Have you got away from God? What a wonderful time it will be for all of us tonight if you come back, back to the foot of the cross, with humble penitent hearts.

1. Philip Hacking's Bible readings in the present volume, p.65

# 'WILL A MAN SERVE GOD FOR NOUGHT?'

*by Dr Ronald Dunn*

## Job 1:9

The verse, the question, that we want to zero in on is this: 'Then Satan answered the Lord, "Does Job fear God for nought?"' Literally – does Job fear God out of favour? Does Job fear God for nothing?

Every time I read that question I am reminded of something that happened some time ago. Early one morning I received a phone call, from an obviously agitated and angry member of my church. After telling me who he was, he blurted out, 'I want you to take my name off the church roll.'

'What!' I demanded.

'I want you to take my name off the church roll,' he said. 'I'm through with it. I'm through with the church, I'm through with God, I'm through with the whole business. Take my name off the church roll.' And immediately I understood what had happened. This man's son, I knew, had gotten into trouble with the law and was on trial, and the man had come to me to talk about the situation, and he'd said, 'Well, I'm a Christian, and I'm praying that God will not let my boy be carried off to jail.' Even though this boy was guilty, he'd done other things as well and he deserved to be punished, yet the father said: 'I'm a Christian; I love God; I am serving God; God's not going to let this happen to my boy.' And so when he called up a few days later and said 'I'm through with it, take my name off the church roll,' I knew what had happened. His son had been found guilty and had been sent to jail. And every time I read this story I am reminded of that man. 'Does Job fear God for nought?'

You see the devil thinks that anyone who worships God is a fool. He says and thinks that the most foolish thing anyone could do would be to love God, to worship and serve Him; to call Jesus Lord would be the height and depth of foolishness and therefore, when he comes across someone who *is* serving God and loving Him, who does follow Jesus Christ as Lord – he is immediately suspicious of his motives.

And that day, as the devil showed up in the courts of heaven, the Lord – and this has always intrigued me – initiated this conversation. I used to wish the Lord would brag about me, until I realised that Job got into all his trouble because the Lord was bragging about him! And the Lord said, 'Hast thou considered my servant Job? There's not another like him on the face of the earth – he loves me, serves me, he turns away from evil. There's nobody like him.'

The devil said, 'Oh yes, I've considered Job. I want to tell you something, God. You've been deceived. You think Job is serving you because he loves you. But he's pulled the wool over your eyes. He's serving you because you've blessed him. You've increased his possessions, put a hedge around him, you've reinforced him – why, of course, the fellow would be a fool not to serve God if he gets that kind of pay cheque! But if you let me get at him, if you take away all that he has, you'll see Job will curse you. Because the only thing Job is serving you for is that it pays to serve you! Will a man serve God for nothing? You think he's serving you because he loves you – you're deceived! If you will remove the hedge and let me strip him of all the blessings, you'll see the truth about Job.'

I think that we would usually say that the theme of the book of Job is, 'Why do Christians suffer?' But to tell the truth, I do not believe that that is the major theme. I think the major question is, 'Why do men serve God?' If you were to strip away all the guarantees of blessing, would you still call Jesus Lord? Would I still follow Him? Would I be as excited about preaching the gospel? Would I still be as excited about worshipping Jesus, and loving Him, if He suddenly turned off the blessings and stripped me of everything? Am I serving God tonight because I know that in doing so, I'm blessed?

I don't know how you do it over here, but once a year many of the churches in the States have what they call a 'stewardship drive', when they try to get all the church members to sign a pledge saying that they'll tithe ten per cent of their income for the next year. Of course all the pastors tell the people how God will make the ninety per cent go further than the hundred per cent did, and of course I believe that the Bible teaches us that God will bless us. But one particular pastor had planned a huge banquet for all his church members, and he'd pushed it and advertised it, and invited another preacher to come in and preach a rousing, stirring stewardship address. I talked to him the day afterwards. 'By the way, how did your stewardship banquet go last night?' He said: 'I don't want to talk about it.' He was so angry. He said, 'Do you know what that fellow told my people last night? After all my preparation, after all the planning, I'd got those folk psyched up to sign on the dotted line, and he got up there and said – People, if you tithe, all I can promise you is that you'll have ten per cent less than before!

But the more I got to thinking the more I wondered. 'What if God didn't bless me?' There's a move on in the States right now to do away with tax credits for gifts to churches. At the moment you can deduct them from your income tax. I've heard preachers say, 'We must fight this – it will destroy the churches. If they take that away, our churches will go under!'

I don't know, folks, but maybe our churches *ought* to go under if that's true . . .

You understand what I'm saying. I believe you should take everything the government gives you. But what I'm saying is: what if the only thing that happened when I obeyed God in the giving of my possessions – was that I gave of my possessions? What if there were no promises? Would I still serve God?

I hate to admit it, but the devil asked a good question.

Three questions. Number one, *Will a man serve God when he is immersed in suffering?* The devil said, 'The reason Job is so faithful in serving you is that you blessed him. Let's see if he finds it so easy to jump up and down and praise the Lord and say hallelujah when he's broke and sick as he does now!' And you know the story. God gave the devil permission to afflict Job, and he was immersed in suffering. Perhaps no man ever suffered like Job suffered. He suffered in his person, and he even suffered in his reputation, because there was a prevalent philosophy in those days that physical blessings were a sign of God's favour; so it went without saying, that if a man has an abundance of blessings and is in good health, then God's blessing him. But if suddenly something happens to that man's fortune and he loses it and he becomes afflicted with all kinds of diseases, there's only one explanation; he's sinned somewhere along the way. The moment Job lost the supposed sign of God's favour, people began to accuse him and question him. 'We always thought that Job was number one citizen . . . but I guess old Job had some secret sins nobody knew about and they finally caught up with him!'

We have in the States what I call the 'joyboys'. They're preachers who go around preaching that if you'll just trust God and be filled with the Spirit you'll always be healthy and wealthy, there'll always be honey, no bees, no work, all ease; you'll be lifted above all the ordinary trials and troubles of life. Being filled with the Spirit is a sort of vaccination that makes you immune to all kinds of problems. I don't know if you have that teaching in this country, but there's quite a bit of it going on today – the idea that if I *really* trust God, if I'm all right with God, then there'll be no unusual difficulties, no hardships, no tragedies, no trials. The only thing wrong with that is that it's wrong! It's not what the Bible teaches.

One of my favourite passages is the eleventh chapter of Hebrews, especially in verse 32 where the author really takes off. 'And what more can I say? For time would fail me to tell of Gideon, Barak, Samson . . . who through faith conquered kingdoms, enforced justice, received promises, stopped the mouths of lions . . . *and others* were tortured . . . suffered markings and scourgings . . . were stoned, sawn in two, were killed with the sword . . . of whom the world was not worthy.' *And others*. I was reading these verses recently and stopped and re-checked. Can that be? Why, I thought that if you had a great faith and knew how to believe God you could move mountains, and you would always be delivered; and suddenly in the middle the author says, 'and others were tortured.' Well, I guess they didn't have as much faith as the other folk . . . there must have been some deep sin hidden in their . . .

No. They had the same kind of faith. You see, the same faith that enables some to escape, enables others to endure. The same faith that delivered from death, enabled others to die. I was talking to someone recently who had been involved in trying to bring healing to somebody, and they said the problem was that the person didn't have enough faith to be healed. May I say to you, I don't think our problem is that we lack the faith to be healed. I think my problem is that I lack the faith to stay sick if that's what God wants. I think I've got enough faith to be healed! – I'm certainly motivated more than anything else, I'd *want* to be healed; but what if God said, 'No. You're to be one of the 'others'. You'll not escape. You must endure.'?

I was reading the story of the three Hebrew children. They're getting ready to throw them into the fiery furnace, and the children say, 'Oh king, we're not worried. Our God is able to deliver us. *But if not . . .*'

Some of us would have to write that under our testimonies. 'But if not . . .' We sometimes say, 'Lord, I don't understand. I call you Lord, I've given myself to serve you, I thought I would get preferential treatment . . .' Will a man serve God for nothing?

And what makes it more painful is that you see others who seem to be just sailing by, they don't know anything of the valleys you've been through and yet you know in your heart they are not as committed to Christ as you are. The psalmist said, 'As for me, my feet had almost slipped away, I said I washed my hands in vain, I've served God for nothing.' It's not as easy to stand up and smile and say 'Jesus is Lord' when you're going down for the third time.

Second question: *Will a man serve God when his friends forsake him?* Job had three friends (at least, that's one opinion). I thank God for friends. You'll never find the word 'saint' in the singular in the New Testament. You know why – God knows we can't live the Christian life by ourselves. We need the mutual encouragement of others. But what happens when friends forsake us? What happens when we can say with Paul, 'Demas has forsaken me, and here I am in the Philippian jail and some of my preaching brethren, they have forsaken me and they're stealing away my members while I'm locked up here . . . All have forsaken me, I'm standing alone'?

When Jesus had that breakfast interview with Peter and restored him, not so much to fellowship (I think that had already taken place) but to his former position of leadership, do you remember, in John 21 He said, 'One of these days they're going to take you where you don't want to go and stretch forth your hands' – this He said to Peter, 'Follow me.' And Peter looked around and he saw John following behind, and Peter said, 'Well, Lord, what about him?' Just like Peter! Just like Ronald Dunn! Just like all of us! 'Yes, I'll follow you — but what's *he* going to do?

And Jesus said, 'If I will that he tarry till I come again that's none of your business. You see to it that you follow me.' And that's still the word that Jesus gives us.

Will a man serve God if he's forsaken by his friends? Will a man stay in a church and minister if nobody seems to appreciate him, and no-one ever comes up and compliments him on the sermon? Will a man serve God? Will a woman? Will a teenager still serve God in school if they stand alone and they're the only ones there, the only ones not doing what's being done? The only ones who are turning down those particular invitations! Nobody else there to comfort and encourage you; you're all by yourself, out there standing alone. Will a man serve God if he's forsaken by his friends?

There's one last question. *Will a man serve God when God is silent?* I think that this is the hardest part of all. You can take just about anything, if you know why. Everywhere I go, every meeting, I'm asked — 'Why?' And that question is always preceded by some story of tragedy or difficulty in the questioner's life. One young pastor said to me, 'God won't tell me why! I could take it if God would just *say* something to me.'

I'm going to tell you something; God will very seldom answer your question of why. It's not that there is no answer, it's just that you and I probably wouldn't be able to comprehend the answer if God were to tell us, and besides that, we have to learn to trust Him without knowing why. We ask Him questions. What we're usually doing is saying 'Lord — explain yourself,' calling God into account. 'All right, I have yielded to the Lordship of Jesus Christ, I've given myself to serving; now Lord, I deserve some consideration, I deserve some answers. I want to know why it is my people don't appreciate me in my

church. I want to know why it is after I've prayed and
prayed, my loved one still died. I want to know why it is
after I've given up a good job to get into the ministry and
do this, I've sacrificed everything, I want to know why it
is, still, Lord, I receive the phone call saying my son's in
jail.' And there's no answer. And that compounds the
heartache.

Well, in closing, I'd like to give you some suggestions
about what to do when God is silent. First thing is; you and
I need to remember that God has a right to be silent. I must
confess to you that when I first started serving Christ and
surrendered my life to the ministry I thought I would get
preferential treatment. I discovered later that there is no
such thing as a charmed life, that even Christians are not
exempt from sufferings. I have a friend I visited, and when
I left he gave me a parting shot: 'Remember – keep loving
God, keep hating sin . . . and watch out for trucks.' Well,
you'd think if you loved God you ought not to have to
watch out for trucks! But what he was saying was that
loving God and hating sin doesn't give you superhuman
power.

Read Job 38. The interesting thing is that when God
finally speaks, He doesn't answer a single one of Job's
questions. All He does is to reassure Job of His own
sovereignty, of His own Lordship, of His own wisdom.
Read chapter 38. God is simply saying, 'Job, I have a right
to do what I've done!'

And I want to say to you, that the Lordship of Jesus
Christ means that I recognise that whatever He does, He
has a *right* to do it. I don't understand it, I may not see the
wisdom or purpose of it, but whatever He does He has a
right to do it. That's what it means to be under the
Lordship of Jesus Christ.

But He has not only a right, He also has a *reason*. Look
at Job 42:1. God has a reason, He has a purpose. I love
that statement of Spurgeon: 'When we cannot trace God's

hand we can trust God's heart.' He is the divine party who always works to a purpose. He has a reason for what He is doing in your life. You say, 'But He didn't answer my prayer!' – God had a reason. 'But He took my loved one!' – God had a reason.

And last, God has a *reward*. I love this! In verse 10, God told Job 'I want you to pray for your friends.'

'Oh yes, Lord. I'll be glad to. Pray you'll bring down fire and brimstone on them, the way they've treated me!'

'No. That's not what I mean. They're in trouble and I want you to pray for them.' Isn't that like God? He said, 'All right, Job; I want you to intercede for your friends.' And the Lord – now, listen – restored the fortunes of Job when he had prayed for his friends. And the Lord gave him twice as much as he had before!

I don't know, but I think we might – ought – to take 'sacrifice' out of the Christian vocabulary. Is it possible for us really to give up anything? God will be no man's debtor! Peter said: 'Lord, what about us? We've left all to follow you.' And Jesus said, 'I tell you, nobody's left houses and land, and husbands and wives, and sons and daughters but that in this life I'll restore them a hundred fold, and in the life to come, life everlasting. Don't talk about what you've given up.' The Lord is no man's debtor.

Folks, God has a reward. 'So the Lord blessed the latter days of Job more than his beginning, and he had fourteen thousand sheep, six thousand camels, a thousand yoke of oxen, a thousand she-asses. And he had also seven sons and three daughters.' Now just a minute – I thought the Bible said the Lord doubled everything Job had, but he started out with seven sons and three daughters and now he has the same.

Well, you see, he didn't have to double those, because he hadn't lost the ones that died. I have a very dear friend whose wife died a few years ago. Somebody said to him, 'I'm sorry you lost your wife.' He said, 'I haven't lost her. I know right where she is.'

> Death can hide but not divide;
> she is on Christ's other side;
> she with Christ and Christ with me,
> united still in Christ are we.

God has a reward. Will a man serve God when God is silent? God has a right to do what He is doing, and He has a reason, and He has a reward.

So the question is – Will a man serve God for nothing? You say, if I were to make some sort of decision tonight that I would commit myself totally to Jesus, does that mean that from now on everything will be wonderful and smooth and glorious? You're not promised that. He is not a bridge over troubled waters, but He is certainly a pathway through them.

Will a man serve God for nothing? The glorious answer that comes back from Job is 'Yes!' And what God was proving to the devil was this: 'Job loves me for myself.'

# 'SEEK YE FIRST
THE KINGDOM OF GOD . . .'

*Rev George Duncan*

## Matthew 6:33

I find that one of the things I'm missing tremendously, now that I no longer have a congregation of my own, is sharing the big moments in the lives of my people – birth, marriage and death. It's such a privileged relationship; I find it very moving when conducting a wedding, to see two young people standing in front of me with their dreams, their hopes and ideals never higher, and their quiet confidence that for them happiness is just around the corner in deeper measure than they've ever known before. But it's not quite as easy as that, and I like to share with them this verse and just speak for five minutes. I can't keep them standing longer than that, or maybe the bride will faint, or something! But tonight I want to expand five minutes to thirty minutes and share this verse with you, because I believe that it says just about everything to ensure firstly, that we are real Christians, not pretend ones; and secondly, that we are the right kind of Christians, and not just any kind.

Was it not interesting that one of the reasons given for the success of British men and forces in the Falkland Islands was the quality of our men? The Argentinian weapons were just as good as ours – if not better; and they had plenty of ammunition. Yet in the end it was our troops who won the day. And it was attributed to the fact that they were trained, they were tougher and better – although some of the Argentinians displayed amazing courage. And I believe that in the spiritual conflict we face today it's the quality of our Christian life that is going to matter: not just, are we Christians? But, what kind of Christians are we? That's the point. And this verse seems to me to indicate that if we really do seek Him with all our heart, this is what is involved when that search finds its objective.

When I talk to a bride and groom I tell them that this is Christ's recipe for happiness in living. What kind of a life will they have together? We're living in rather tragic days, aren't we? So many marriages that begin with high hopes end in despair. That's why in my travels around the country I find that the section of the community that is seeking God possibly more than any other, is the section we call the 'young marrieds'. They see so many marriages ending in divorce and disaster and misery, they don't want their marriage to end that way; and they're seeking help.

Then what is involved, if we finally find Him whom we seek? I want to suggest that this recipe – which bears a divine guarantee, not a human one – involves three very simple things; they're not at all complicated. First, it speaks of

## The presence of the King

You can't have a kingdom without a king; you can't be a Christian without having Christ. May I just lay down that fundamental note, because it's just possible that there's someone here and you haven't yet grasped the simplest and most basic fact of Christian experience – that it has to do with Jesus Christ. More than the church, the creeds, more than a code of conduct, it has to do with Him. You see, the Christian life is Christ's life being lived out in me by His Spirit. This is what my Bible says: 'This is the record; that God hath given to us eternal life and this life is in His Son.

He that hath not the Son hath not the life.' And the presence of the King, which is the first essential in this recipe, is something I dare not leave out.

Before I left St George's, Troon, in Glasgow, I got a letter from a teenage girl asking for help. When our Women's Guild had their annual sale of work, I never liked to ask the church to do anything unless I did something too, so I made what I always love to make – not very good for the figure – chocolate fudge. And this girl wrote to me just before I left, and said, 'Dear Mr Duncan – before you go, do you think you could let me have your recipe for chocolate fudge?' So I said, 'I'll be very happy to do that, indeed I'll do better; I'll come round and I'll show you how to make it, if you buy the ingredients.' I listed them for her; and my last visit to that home was spent largely in the kitchen making fudge, but it didn't go right! I kept on letting it simmer and testing it – you know, you test it in a saucer of cold water and you wait for it to harden into a firm lump. But it wouldn't harden, and I went on and on, and the clock ticked on and on. Finally I turned to the girl and asked, '*Was* that butter you gave me?' She replied, 'No – it was margarine!' And I said, 'Well, that explains it.'

I must add that it did come right after that, but my wrists were nearly broken by the time I'd beaten and beaten and beaten it. You see, we hadn't got the right ingredient. And I believe a lot of people in their so-called Christian experience go all wrong because they haven't got Christ.

Two things are involved here. First,

## My acceptance of that presence

I have to accept Christ into my life by His Spirit. I remember the testimony of Dr W I Fullerton, the Irish Baptist; 'The gift of God is eternal life.' A gift is yours when you take it; and, said Dr Fullerton with his beaming face, 'I took it and it's mine because I took it.'

Have you taken Christ into your life? Until you have, you're not a Christian. You may be a member of a church, and I don't care what the label is, you're not a Christian. 'He that hath the Son hath the life; he that hath not the Son hath not the life.' I was just eleven-and-a-half, a minister's son, baptised as a baby, went to church every Sunday (never to Sunday School but always to church), read my Bible, said my prayers when I remembered; and I had to learn that none of those things made me a Christian. Only one thing would, and that would be if I welcomed Christ into my life. And as a small boy, scarcely knowing what it meant, I accepted the king.

I wonder if you've seen that lovely painting in St Paul's Cathedral – Holman Hunt's *Christ, the Light of the World*. The familiar words: 'Behold I stand at the door and knock; if any man hear my voice and open the door, I will come in.' I've heard some theologians pour scorn on that – Christ as a sort of feeble, weak supplicant waiting at the door when to them He is sovereign Lord. But He is also full of grace. When a king stands waiting and knocking and waits for you, that's grace. And He is full of grace. Have you accepted Him? I wonder whether there's some person here, you've been trying to live the Christian life and you haven't got it. You need to accept Him.

*My assurance of that presence*

Can I be really sure that I am a Christian? Well, the Bible says we can be sure. 'These things have I written unto you that you might have eternal life.' Coming from north of the border I'm very well aware of the canniness of the Scots of the Western Highlands and Islands. I think of a godly old man; if ever a man was a Christian he was; but if you were to ask him, 'Are you a Christian?', he would never venture beyond 'I'll be hoping so.' Does God want us just to hope? The Bible says we can *know*! If I asked you whether you were married, and you said, 'Well, I'll be hoping so,' I would begin to wonder whether you really knew what you were talking about! No, there is no presumption when we are just resting on God's assured and pledged Word. It is presumption to doubt.

'Seek ye *first* the kingdom' – that speaks to me of

## The priority of the King

My brother had the privilege of staying at Balmoral and preaching before Her Majesty the Queen. And there were certain very strict rules of court etiquette – some of them, I think, designed to preserve the sanity, if not the life, of the Queen. One of these rules was that if there was to be conversation between the Queen and a commoner, the Queen spoke first (knowing my brother's capacity for conversation, I think that's possibly a very wise thing!). You see it's not just a matter of having the right ingredients; you've got to do things in the right order.

When we used to take our scouts to camp on Windybrow, on the side of Latrigg here in the Lake District, we used to allow a different patrol to do the cooking each day. They didn't know much about cooking, so either the Scoutmaster or the Assistant Scoutmaster (I was the assistant) would be in charge of the cooking. It was thought we might know a fraction more than they did. Of course, when it was my turn to decide on the menu I chose chocolate pudding. You couldn't possibly go wrong – all the instructions were on the side of the packet. You couldn't *possibly* go wrong. Or could you? You see, the instructions on the cornflour made it clear that you mix it with *cold* milk. First you set aside some cold for the cornflour, then you heat the rest. But try to mix the cornflour with hot milk, and you're in trouble.

Well, we didn't save some cold milk first. We heated it all and mixed the cornflour with hot. The result; the most unattractive, sticky, glutinous, lumpy kind of chocolate pudding I've ever eaten in my life. There was nothing wrong with the ingredients; we'd got all the right ones; but they were not in the right order. And I want to suggest to you that the basic problem in Christian living today is very often not that we haven't got the right ingredients, but that we're not giving priority to the King.

You see, in my life there can be

## Alternatives to the will of God

Do you remember how Paul wrote to the church at Ephesus? It was a wicked old city. The whole temple of Diana was just a sink of iniquity. The priestesses were prostitutes. It was a vile place. And there, God planted a church; and Paul, writing to the Ephesian Christians in that tough situation reminded them how they used to live before they became believers. 'Do you remember? You used to do what everybody else did. You walked according to the course of this world.' And that is one of the alternatives. You can do what everybody else does.

I feel desperately sorry for young people growing up in today's world where standards have almost all been eroded. Even in Christian circles they're going by the board. 'Well, he does it; she does it; it's all right.' Well, is it? How do you know? Paul said, 'You lived a life in which you fulfilled the desires of the flesh and the mind.' You did what other people did; you did what you wanted. These things are past now as determining factors. Oh, sometimes you will do what others do, sometimes what you want; but these things are never decisive. How do you know that the thing you want is right? How do you know? I've never forgotten a lovely old chap I met in Edinburgh who told me, 'Mr Duncan, for thirty years I haven't darkened the door of a church.' And then he added, 'And for thirty years I've been wrong.'

Thirty years wasted. How *do* you know what is right? How do you know that what everybody else does is right? No, there are alternatives to the will of God.

## Authority in the will of God

It is *His* will. You see, He's not only Saviour and friend, He is Lord. That figure in Holman Hunt's picture is wearing a crown. He is King; in mercy, in grace, He stands and waits. We've no business to keep Him waiting, though in grace He waits. But He is wearing a crown, and He is Lord.

I recall that when the 'Jesus Movement' first hit the United States, it made a terrific impact. Like every movement it had extremes and unbalances, but at the centre there was a reality; young people believing that Jesus has the answer. *Time* magazine was so impressed that it devoted an eight-page colour spread to the 'Jesus People'. I can only remember one of the pictures. It was of a girl with her back to the camera, and on her red sweater were the words 'Jesus is my Lord'. I thought, what incredible courage to go around wearing that. Jesus is Lord; and whether or not we wear it outside, we have to wear it inside, because He is – or is He?

Punctuation is not inspired in the Bible; there is no punctuation in the original Greek. Sometimes it makes quite a difference, for example in that very well known verse, 'By grace are you saved . . .' I think I prefer the old rendering to that of the New International Version, which supplies a comma where there isn't one in my Authorised Version. 'By grace are you saved through faith' – that's what grace has done; made salvation depend on faith, because we couldn't keep the law.

But there's another verse where punctuation makes a great difference. Do you remember when Saul of Tarsus was met by the risen Christ, and he fell down to the earth blinded? And he lay there and heard a voice saying, 'Saul, Saul, why persecutest thou me?' Do you remember that? And do you remember how, in his bewilderment, he replied: 'Who art thou Lord?' That's how my Authorised Version puts it. The question mark comes at the end. I wonder whether that's right? I would like to shift that question mark forward: 'Who art thou?' – pause – 'Lord!' And back comes the confirming word, 'You're right; I am Jesus whom you persecute.' Saul recognised right away that Jesus was King. I think one of the loveliest of the modern choruses is one that I love, but I tremble when I hear it sung:

> He is Lord, He is Lord,
> He is risen from the dead and He is Lord;
>      Every knee shall bow,
>      Every tongue confess
> That Jesus Christ is Lord.

When I hear that I am reminded of Jeremy Taylor's first rule for holy living – 'Don't lie to God'. He insists on being Lord. It's the priority of the King. It means that in every situation, in every area of my life, I don't say 'What do other people think?' or say 'What do I want?'; but I say what Saul said; 'Lord, what do you want me to do?'

**The promise of the King**

It's so wonderful – 'All these needful things will be added unto you' – necessary things, not luxuries. That speaks of two things. Firstly,

*An abundance that will meet my every need*
You see this is a life in which it's rather like a pauper marrying a millionaire. There will be big demands made, but the resources are there.

An American preacher once spoke of Christians who had 'run out of gas'. I wonder if there's a Christian here who's 'run out of gas' – it may be in your marriage, it may be in your life. It's not necessary, when we have all that there is in Christ. You see there's much, much more than forgiveness in this Christ of ours. Oh, of course it begins there, at the cross; Christ for me! But more than that it's Christ *in* me, Christ *through* me. A verse we often apply to heaven has in fact nothing really to do with heaven. Do you remember, Paul writes 'Eye hath not seen, nor ear heard, nor hath entered into the heart of man the things that God hath prepared for those that love Him.' That's not heaven. He goes on, 'But God hath revealed them unto us by His Spirit.' And when Paul tries to think of the wonder of the sufficiency of God's grace he just runs out of words. We're not wise enough, but He is; we're not loving enough, but He is; we're not brave enough, but He is; everything we lack, He has. And He's dwelling in my heart by His Spirit. An abundance that will meet my every need in life and in death.

*An abundance that will mark my daily life*
If you married a millionaire I think you would dress maybe slightly differently. You might have a different car. It wouldn't make any difference to the millionaire. And I don't think any millionaires worry about the size of their telephone bills, because they have plenty of resources. And you and I have all we need in Christ.

Dr Graham Scroggie's definition of peace was 'the possession of adequate resources'. That's why I think this verse comes at the end of a passage in which our Lord has been talking about not worrying. If we have Him, if we put Him first, He's going to take care of everything we need.

There was a time in my life when we were really in financial difficulty. I was in a church, I was raising a family, and my problem was of course that I didn't have enough money to raise the family and run the car. It wasn't too difficult to solve the problem. I couldn't sell the kids! So I sold the car . . . That raised another problem. Now I couldn't do my work. Well, the time came when I was moving on and I had a phone call from a very delightful lady who had two cars; in those days if you had two cars you really had a bank balance. I answered the phone and she said, 'I know you want to visit the congregation, and you know I have two cars. I want you to have my Wolseley and that'll help you to visit the congregation.'

Well, I knew that car. It was a monstrous size and it drank petrol by the gallon. So I thanked her very much and didn't do anything about it. A week later the phone rang again. 'You haven't done anything about my car.'

'No,' I said, 'I'm afraid I haven't.'

'I don't think you understand,' she said. 'It won't cost you a penny. I'll pay for petrol, garage, any repairs.'

Well, that was different, wasn't it? And for I think the only time in my life I ran a car without anxiety. I was running it on her bank balance, and I knew it could cope.

That's a wonderful way to life, isn't it? And I think it's the way we're all meant to live.

> When first before His mercy seat
> Thou didst to Him thine all commit
> He gave thee warrant from that hour
> To trust His wisdom, love and power.

What a way to live! Is that your pattern? Is that your recipe? Is that your way? If you seek Him with all your heart you're going to find Him. And you need Him.

# HE IS LORD – IS HE YOURS?

*by Rev Philip Hacking*

## Genesis 28:10-22

I'm afraid I seem to have got stuck in Genesis this week! But not the first eleven chapters tonight, but chapter 28, to show us there's a little bit more to the book. We are going to look at a man who was in a storm. And the concern that I have on my heart tonight is that it's one thing for God to bring us through the storm, and through the storm to Jesus – that I guess all or most of us here can testify to. But even a storm doesn't in itself bring you to Jesus. There's something you've got to do in that storm.

I can remember as a very little lad (I want to emphasise, as a *very* little lad), I was at church at the time of Dunkirk. I know you can't really believe that I was alive then – appearances are deceptive! I remember being in that church with my mother, and I was old enough at least to notice that the church was suddenly much fuller than I'd ever seen it before, and I asked my mother where they'd all come from. 'It's Dunkirk,' she said. 'We're praying.' Next Sunday I was back in church and I asked her where they had all gone to, because they were not there any more. And you see, this to me is the kind of parable that is all too often true. We have in our church – as many of you do, no doubt – leaflets that we give out about praying for people. Of course, we pray for people in need. Here's someone who has been bereaved, here's someone who has been ill, someone facing redundancy, someone who's got exams – we pray for them by name, yes. But I want to draw up a list, for example, 'Will you pray for Mr John Smith? Everything is going well for him, he's got a marvellous bank balance, he's on top of the world . . . Pray for him, he's probably in greater need than the person who's going to have an operation next week.'

And I want to say to you that it may be that you're here tonight on this lovely evening and your heart is full of joy, and there are not any obvious storms, or you've passed through the storms; and you have still not found Jesus as the Lord of your life.

Take a journey with me back to Jacob, and I hope that by the end of this evening something will have happened of real significance.

I assume a fair knowledge of the story. If you don't know it well, perhaps you'll read it later. Let me point out to you, it's the nearest equivalent you'll get in an Old Testament story to a conversion experience in the New Testament. It's almost like Saul on the Damascus road. It's a very great turning point in Jacob's life. You will say, if you know the story, 'But it's only the beginning!' Yes, only the beginning. Jacob didn't become Israel overnight. There was a lot to follow, a great wrestling in the thirty-second chapter and a lot more had to go on, before Jacob became Israel.

I don't know about you, but I have to confess I don't particularly like Jacob, he's not one of my favourite biblical characters. Maybe it's because I see too much of myself in him. He really wasn't all that wonderful, was he? And he really did need changing, didn't he. And yet the marvellous thing about the story of Jacob is that over the years this man who was a deceiver and whose name-word meant 'deceiver' was changed into one who was a prince, and wrestled with God, whose name the people of Israel still hold on to.

It all happened over a long period, but there was a moment when something dramatic happened. In a sense, nothing in a convention can happen which, like a package deal, can change all the thousands here tonight. Of course not. It would be possible that there might be such a moving of the Spirit of God, that many people would go out with an awareness that something had happened. But the proof that it had would be seen in the days that lie ahead. The storm may have its place; but you prove it's real when you're the other side of the storm. But all we can be sure about is what happens tonight. And for Jacob, Bethel, that house of God, was a place he never forgot. Maybe this tent in Keswick in 1982 will be a place we shall never forget. So let's look at the story. I am terribly traditional by nature, and so I have just three points for you tonight. The first,

## He was a man who knew his need (verses 10-12)

Jacob, with all his faults, when he met with God unexpectedly that night knew what kind of need he had. I hope that's true of you. What was his need? Well, there was

### *The past and its failures*

Why I don't like Jacob very much is that he really was a bit of a rotter, that he could deceive his old blind father as he did – even a pagan shouldn't behave like that, least of all a spiritually-minded man. And he could deceive Esau of his birthright – well, that's a little less dodgy, because Esau was a very worldly man. But Jacob had a conscience, as he came to that place and put the stone for his pillow and lay down to sleep. He was wrestling with his conscience like Paul on the Damascus road.

Maybe we drag something of that with us; an awareness that all has not been well in the past. Now I don't think we preach anything special at Keswick except the Word of God. But there has been a kind of traditional programme for the week's teaching that we follow, and I believe it to be helpful. So at this point in the week we've been reminded of the sin in our life, reminded that Jesus made provision for our need; and tomorrow we shall be reminded of the coming of the Holy Spirit and the fullness of the Spirit to enable us. And here we stand today, in between, conscious of our need. Perhaps we've come to Keswick unhappy about the past and its failures. Now I want to tell you tonight, that as you meet with the Lord this evening, as He really becomes Lord of your life, whatever the past may be that's lingering on and making you hamstrung in the Lord's service, it can be put behind you. Paul speaks in Philippians 3:13 about 'forgetting what lies behind'. That's a good thing. But first of all, get it dealt with; the past and its failures.

But the second thing was,

### The future and its fears

Jacob was a timid soul. He was a terribly spoilt lad; you know the story, his mother spoilt him terribly. Now he was going out to the vast unknown. He'd made a mess in the past and he really couldn't be sure that the God his father and grandfather talked about would be with him in that unknown place to which he went. He stepped out into the unknown; and as he lay there that night, something dramatic happened. There was a ladder stretched up to heaven (verse 12). It was right where he was. And suddenly it dawned upon Jacob that wherever he was, at any moment, the ladder was there and the Lord was above it.

That's the real possibility for you; the awareness of a truth that I guess you've known for years. As you step into an unknown future, there's a ladder stretched up to heaven. You don't have to turn the clock back, it's here. May I say in parenthesis, it's true of our nation. I don't think we have to go back to some bygone age to find revival. The ladder is here. It's in our midst. It's not a case of God doing again what He did years and years ago. It's

God where we are now, doing a new thing. You can't turn the clock back in your life, or in Keswick, or in Britain. And for Jacob, he knew his need; and there was a ladder.

## He was a man who met his Lord there (verses 12-16)

What he saw was a ladder stretched between earth and heaven. You may remember Jesus spoke of this at the end of John 1 to Nathanael – it's a lovely link. But there at that moment two things gave him strength. One was

### The presence of the Lord

Just look at verse 13. 'I am the Lord, the God of your father Abraham and the God of Isaac.' Not yet the God of Jacob, not yet. 'The God of Abraham and the God of Isaac and I'm here and I've got a promise for you' – but first, it was the presence of the Lord. We pray very earnestly on this platform that somehow through our words, with all their shortcomings, the heavens will in some measure open and you'll see something. What we trust is not the gifts of God, but the Lord Himself. And the message that comes through is 'I am the God of Abraham and Isaac, your father, your grandfather, but I remain in the present. All else changes; I am the same.'

The second thing was

### The promise of the Lord

What did the Lord promise? He promised him first of all that He'd give him the land; secondly, that He'd watch over his family; and perhaps most of all (verse 15) 'I am with you and will watch over you wherever you go, and I will bring you back.' That's great, isn't it? 'I am with you'. Think how often that promise comes in Scripture; to Joshua, facing the task of leading the people of God; to Gideon; to the disciples, facing the enormous challenge, 'Go, make disciples of all nations.' And whatever the Lord may be asking of *you* these days at Keswick – 'I am with you, I'll keep you wherever you go.'

The presence of the Lord; the promise of the Lord. Now, I hope you're listening carefully.

In a sense, I've said the kind of thing perhaps you expected me to say, and maybe it all sounds very trad and very usual and the sort of thing you might expect on a Wednesday at Keswick; and at this point we could go out of this tent and we could all say, 'Yes – it's great, He's with us in the storm, He's with us wherever we go, He's made His promise.' But you see He wants *you* to do something about it.

So my last point is my main point:

### He is a man who made his mark (verses 16-22)

I do not understand the game of rugby; it is a mysterious and wonderful game to me. I've tried, from time to time, to understand the rules. It seems to me you just kick the ball as far as you can and everybody applauds like mad. I've never understood why that was so wonderful! But anyway occasionally I listen to the commentary and I hear the man get very excited. All I can see is a whacking great chap standing there, and everybody tries to knock him off his feet, and this chap digs his heel into the ground and the commentator rises to a great crescendo. 'He's made his mark!' And we're all very excited about it. He's dug a bit of the turf out and everybody is thrilled!

All the rugby players will have me written off by now . . . I'm sorry about that . . . but apparently what's happened is that this man has dug his heel in, and whatever happens now he gets a kick. He's made his mark. He's said, 'I'm here!'

Five hundred years ago this year a great man of God was born: Martin Luther. And Martin Luther is said to have made his stand and declared, 'Here I stand; I can do no other.' A stand. Now, it's this that I want all of us to feel tonight. 'I'm going to make a mark. I'm not just going to say, yes, it's true, the Lord is wonderful, He's made His promise; I'm going to make a mark.'

What mark did Jacob make? Just look at these last few verses. The first mark when he woke up from this dramatic dream was *an act of adoration*. He actually started by worshipping that great God. In the Bible, when people meet their God, it's not marvellous and exciting, it's awesome. Isaiah in the temple, Peter by the lakeside – afraid. Jacob felt like that; and if tonight you've made your mark, you won't go away shouting, you'll go away stilled. You see, the Lord mattered. 'This is the house of God – this is the gate of heaven.'

He worshipped. He rose early in the morning, and he took the stone, and he worshipped. I hope that one of the ways you'll make your mark tonight is with a new sense of adoration to call Jesus Lord; to acknowledge Him as Lord. Nobody ever *made* Him Lord. When I was young I was told I had to make Him Lord; I understand what they meant but I think they were wrong. He *is* Lord. I can't make or unmake Him. Whatever I do with Him tonight, He's Lord! If everybody in this audience rejected Him, He'd still be Lord.

To acknowledge Him as such means that you worship Him. And if it's a real experience it will mean an adoration and a worship that will spill out day after day, in the years that lie ahead.

Secondly, there was *a dedication* when he made his mark. If you look at verses 20 and 21, at first sight it seems like a kind of bargain, doesn't it. I'm sure it doesn't mean that. All he's saying in verses 20 and 21 is, 'Lord, I believe what you've promised and on the assumption that what you've promised is true, and I accept it, then the Lord shall be my God.' You cannot bargain with God. He does not work on the bargain system. You take Him at His word; you believe Him. And you say to Him, 'My Lord and my God.'

I was always very fond of dear Thomas, ever since I was rector at a church called St Thomas's. He was a great man, at least an honest one; and when he'd wrestled with his doubts and his problems he came to the place where he said, 'My Lord and my God'. You remember, he found it hard to believe.

I remember in my church at Sheffield one night a Canadian post-graduate student came with a question after a guest service. I answered his question, and he went away. Next Sunday, he came back, asked another question and then went away. When he came back the third Sunday, I thought 'Oh, he's one of those who are always asking questions.' I did my best again. On the fourth Sunday he reappeared and I began to think up ways of avoiding him. But he came up to me and this time he said, 'Thank you for answering my questions. I now believe He is risen from the dead and He is my Lord. I want you to know.'

He became one of the most dedicated Christians we ever had in our church. A remarkable young man. But like Thomas, he had to go through with it; did Jesus rise from the dead? Can you trust Him? Right, then; the Lord is my God. And, do you see, that's the point of dedication. He's the God of your fathers, He's the God of Martin Luther, the God of this convention – but is He your Lord? My Lord; my God.

There's one last thing, and I hope it doesn't sound like an anti-climax – I hope it's going to be the climax. There was an adoration; there was a dedication; but Jacob made his mark in the most practical way. There were two *demonstrations*. The first was, he raised a pillar. The patriarchs were always raising little cairns, and they would go back to them and it would remind them that there they made their mark. I don't know what the District Council of Keswick would think, if all of you started raising cairns outside! But think of it metaphorically; that you stand up and are not ashamed to say, 'This is my Lord.'

Do you remember how a little lady was healed in a remarkable way? She touched the hem of Jesus' garment. And Jesus said, 'Who touched me?' And this woman came out, says Mark, trembling, terrified. And Jesus said, 'Go in peace; your faith' – not 'my garment' – 'has made you whole.' Not just healed you of an issue of blood, but made you whole. And kind, loving Jesus made that terrified woman stand up in front of a crowd, terrified, but oh, she was so glad she did!

It's not a thing we do so much nowadays and I don't expect I'll do it tonight, but I do want to say that there is a rightful place for nailing your colours to the mast and saying 'My Lord, and My God'. My mark.

But there's the other demonstration, and this is the costly one. Jacob said, 'Whatever you give me, I'll give the tenth.' Now that may seem an awful anti-climax. Maybe I should have preached this before, not after, the collection! But here was Jacob saying, 'I want to show you in practical terms, you are my Lord.' Do you remember the story of Zacchaeus? If you read the story carefully, it doesn't tell you how he was converted. But one thing we do know. He said 'Half of my goods I give, and whatever I've taken wrong, I'll give them back four-fold.' And then Jesus said, 'Salvation has come to this house.'

I think the Lord is saying to a lot of people who make a kind of mark, 'I want you to show it's real.' It was on this platform that I dared to say, more than ten years ago, that anyone who spends more on their annual holiday than they give to the work of God overseas is a hypocrite. I mean that. Anyone can sing 'He is Lord, He is risen from the dead and He is Lord', and we can get very excited about it and sway and lift our hands. But God's not bothered about how you sing; it's how you live. And I believe that the Lord wants me to say – and I say it to my own congregation so I say it to every Christian person here who says 'Jesus is Lord' – it's got to be seen with what you do with your money, your time, your talents, your possessions. Would anyone guess that He was Lord?

A biographer of the Duke of Wellington discovered some old cheque stubs belonging to him. 'When I saw how he spent his money,' he said, 'I knew the man.' Supposing all you left behind when you went to glory was your cheque book. Suppose I did. Would they say, Philip Hacking loved Jesus more than anything else? I wonder. Dedication is not what you do with your hymn book, it's what you do with your cheque book. If that's an anti-climax, so be it. But I just want to say that I know it is Jesus who says to us, 'Not everyone who calls me Lord, Lord, shall enter; but he who does the will of my Father, who is in heaven. Is He Lord?

Would you dare tonight to make your mark? The storms have brought you to Jesus, you've come aware of your needs, you've met Him and His promise and His presence. And you want to say 'Right, Lord. In view of all you've done for me and mean to me, I mean business.'

There's a world outside where the enemy of souls has got his millions who mean business. And when the Christian church means business, we shall win. But not before. I trust you will dare to make your mark and demonstrate it tonight.

'He is Lord!' . . . Is He yours?

# SIN, AND WHAT TO DO WITH IT

*by Rev Tom Houston*

I am a little afraid in approaching this subject, that one might have the experience that I heard about a minister having some time ago. After he had been just a short time in a new church, one of his congregation, ostensibly trying to assure him and affirm him, shook his hand after the service and said: 'Pastor, we didn't know what sin was until you came'!

I had a professor at university who used frequently to tell the story of a man who went into a church and sat near a stained-glass window on which were the ten commandments. 'You know,' he said to himself, 'this should be like an examination paper; attempt only five . . .' Now that story is symptomatic of where society is today. Sin is not high on the charts of what interests people or what even concerns them today. I want to begin by emphasising that, because it is the context out of which we have all come into this meeting.

A remarkable study is currently going on in ten countries in Europe and is now extending to take in the United States, Canada, Japan, Costa Rica, South Korea and a number of other countries. It began as the 'European values study'. A number of things are coming to light about all these countries and particularly our own. A representative sample of people in this country was asked whether they believed in sin. 69 per cent said 'Yes', the number saying 'No' was 25 per cent, and the 'don't knows' were another 6 per cent. That means that 3 out of every 10 people in this country do not believe in sin, or don't know whether they do or not. Then another question that was put to our countrymen was this, about good and evil: 'Do you believe that there are absolutely clear guidelines about what is good and what is evil?' The number saying 'Yes' to that was only 28 per cent. 69 per cent – 2 out of 3 – said that it depends on the circumstances. Now this is the context out of which tonight we come to consider 'The hindrances to holiness', which is our theme for the day. We are going to consider the subject, coming from a society that is pressing in the opposite direction.

Let me illustrate how this is working out. Again from this study; do you know the single thing which we British believe to be the least justifiable act a person can commit? To take and drive away somebody else's car. I'll give you the first ten in that list of least justifiable things to give you some idea of the society in which we are living. Second, was accepting a bribe; third, claiming State benefits to which you are not entitled; fourth, threatening workers who refuse to strike; fifth, taking marijuana; sixth, fighting the police; seventh, political assassination; eighth, having sex with people under the age of consent; ninth, buying stolen goods; and tenth, avoiding paying your fare on public transport.

Now I've gone through the first ten of the list of things that this sample reckoned to be the least justified acts that people can commit. I wonder if you have noticed anything significant? Not one of them is one of the ten commandments.

How do I speak to you tonight, to show you that what our society is saying to us is wrong? Well, my Bible tells me that it is the work of the Holy Spirit to convict people of sin, and the instrument He uses is the Bible, the Word of God. I want to take an Old Testament parable tonight, a winsome story told by one friend to another to put him right when he was wrong. It is found in 2 Samuel chapter 12. The friend who spoke was a man called Nathan. He was a prophet and spoke in the name of God. The person to whom he spoke was a king. His name was David. Twice in the Old Testament, once in the New, David is called 'a man after God's own heart who fulfilled all His will'. But as you read the story of David you realise that there is an oscillating pattern in the graph of his development. It's worth recognising that there were ups and downs in this man's life, down times which were always a prelude to rising higher.

We find David at a point where his relationship with God takes a serious plunge. It stays low for about one year and then rises again. This is the story of how he got his eighth wife, Bathsheba, and by her, his son and successor, Solomon the king.

We know how David came by three of his wives. The first was Michal, the daughter of Saul. He went with his men and killed two hundred Philistines and brought their foreskins to her father. For the second of his wives he was scarcely prevented from the massacre of all the males on a farm which had 4,000 head of cattle; but conveniently the husband, Nabal, went into a coma and died ten days later. And almost before the heat was out of the corpse, David wooed and won Abigail, his second wife. The next five are mainly names. We gather that he had some concubines also; but the last and the eighth of his wives was Bathsheba. That is the context in which we are going to read. I wanted you to have the facts, so that you do not see this story as an isolated incident. It is more than that. And just in case you are not familiar with the Old Testament let me fill in the rest of the facts. David took this Bathsheba – she must have been young; and she was the granddaughter of Ahithopel, his most trusted counsellor. She was the wife of one of the picked officers in his personal bodyguard.

David took her and made her pregnant. Then he un-
successfully tried to cover up the matter by trying to make
her husband Uriah seem the natural father, and when that
didn't work he arranged for Uriah to be killed in battle and
took her – now technically a widow – as his eighth wife.
Those are the bare facts.

Let us look now at the parable in 2 Samuel 12. What do
we learn about what sin is, from this story? Sin is to take
what belongs to another. 'He took the poor man's lamb.'
It is to be not content with what is properly your own.
What we take may belong to God or to other people, but
sin is of this nature. in your mind, check the ten
commandments; they are all theft of one kind or another.
Sin is not to be content with what is properly your own,
and to take from God or man.

The second thing we find about sin in this parable is that
sin is to lack compassion. Verse 6: he had no pity. Sin is to
fail to put ourselves sympathetically in the place of the
other person who is affected. Not to think about God, and
its effect on God; not to think about the other person and
its effect on him. In other words, sin is, not to love our
neighbour as ourselves.

Thirdly, Nathan goes on to point out in verses 7 and 8,
sin is ingratitude for what you have. David, for all the
abundance he had received, was not grateful. As so often is
the case, the essence of sin is an unthankful heart.
Ingratitude for all that we have, still wanting more because
we don't have a pause in our lives to thank God for what
He has given us.

Fourthly, sin is to lack a sense of proportion. This man
had many cattle and sheep. The other man had just one
ewe lamb. And when we get into the syndrome that makes
us sin, we lose the sense of proportion and we do
something that will benefit us no more than adding five
pence to a million-pound fortune. For that was all that the
man was doing in the story; and so often, when we are
violating the law of God, we are just valuing the moment

and having no regard for the whole of life, ours or others.

The fifth thing in this story about sin is that sin is to despise God and His word. Three times it comes. Verse 9: 'Why have you despised the word of the Lord?' said Nathan to his friend. But sin is not just despising the word of God. Verse 10, and again verse 14 – 'Nevertheless, by this deed you have utterly scorned the Lord.' Sin is to despise God and His word, to think that you know better than God, that you have greater vision than the Bible. I'm grateful to Nathan for bringing this word from God to his friend David. For I learn a lot here about sin that makes me wise. Sin is to be discontented and rob another, to lack compassion, to stifle gratitude, to lose a sense of proportion, to despise God and His word.

That's what sin is.

Let me go on, to speak what *not* to do with sin. First of all, don't cover up by stepping up righteousness in other areas. That was the first thing David tried to do. He had sinned against Bathsheba and he tried to be nice to Uriah. He had sinned against Bathsheba and when Nathan came with his parable David got on his judgement seat. What a great judge he was being at that point! And sometimes that's the way we deal with sin. We try to ignore it and step up our righteousness in other areas. One of the commonest ways we do it is to become self-righteous. We crusade to change people and society, and all the time it is just a drive to face away from the thing that is in our hearts.

Second thing not to do: don't try to remove one sin by committing another. First it was adultery, then murder, and in between, a good deal of lying. Sometimes when we get caught sinning, the worst thing we can imagine is to get found out. So we take steps not to be found out and that makes us sin again. Don't do it. Don't compound it.

The third thing not to do is to get someone to cover up for you. David got Joab to cover up for him and take care of Uriah at the battlefront, to see that he got killed in the fighting. Look it up. You will find that David was in Joab's power for ever after that. Alexander Whyte says that Joab said to himself, 'Yes, he can compose and sing psalms with the best of them; but when he wants a bit of dirty work done, it's to me that he comes.' So if there is sin, don't get someone to cover for you, or you will come under their power also.

The fourth thing not to do about sin is to delay dealing with it. It was the best part of a year before David took any action, and not until his friend came. A child had been born in the meantime; everything seemed to be going all right. And yet when he writes about it in the 32nd psalm we know it is not so. 'When I declared not my sin my body wasted away through my groaning . . .' He was trying to say it was all right, but his nervous system, his emotional reactions, his body, was telling a different story. So don't delay in dealing with sin, for David goes on to say that 'when he acknowledged his sin to God and did not hide his iniquity, then you forgave.'

What are we to do with sin? Well, I think that Alec Motyer is going to deal with that, but I've just one or two things to add from the story.

Firstly, cultivate at least one person who will be gently honest with you when you do sin. I think it is tremendous that David the king had Nathan the prophet as his friend. Someone who would gently level with him. Oh, happy the person who has someone with whom they are in such a relationship of friendship that they will tell them.

In the East African revival they use the word 'challenge'. If you are a brother in revival, yes, it means you will confess your sin to one another, but it equally means that you will challenge your brother in love. That's one of the things we do about sin. But then it goes on; we need to admit it, and we need to accept its consequences. I find as I deal with my own heart and as I counsel others, this is the work of repentance. When a person is really prepared to accept the consequences of their own sin, whether they have to or not; and it's at two levels. The eternal level — we have to realise that the consequence of our sin is death, eternal death. When we accept that as a consequence, then we are ready to believe and understand why Jesus had to die on the cross, the just for the unjust, so that He could bring us to God. But it is also at the here and now level: and I believe that the mark of repentance is to be prepared to accept the consequences of your sin if God should so require. To trust in His mercy. And so often, He is merciful.

What to do with sin? Cultivate people who will level with you; admit it quickly, accept its consequences; and cast yourself on the mercy of God.

And the last thing. Get up after you have been forgiven, and live again, by the mercy of God. You will find at the end of the story that the child dies. David accepts this and he goes out to live again and to be the man again that he has been before. And this is the last incident where we have David's wiving tendency getting in the way. That's why I believe it was told at length, because it was the time when he was delivered once and for all of this thing that had dogged his life. So the last thing to do, once we have come for the forgiveness of God, is to arise and live again by the mercy of God. Amen.

# 'I ACKNOWLEDGE MY TRANSGRESSIONS'

## by Rev Alec Motyer

*This address followed that given by Rev Tom Houston, which precedes it in the present volume.*

## Psalm 51

When you see the heading of this psalm you will think that Mr Houston and I had our heads together for a long time, but I want to say that it's heads in heaven that have been together, not on earth – we both came to Keswick previously prepared and committed to these passages. How marvellous that in the over-ruling of God, we come to a psalm bearing the heading *A psalm of David when Nathan the prophet came to him after he had gone into Bathsheba.*

We read in the psalm, 'Have mercy upon me, Oh God, according to thy lovingkindness; according to the multitude of thy compassions, blot out my transgressions.' Look out for that word 'blot out', it is going to come again in our reading. In the beginning of verse 2, 'Wash me thoroughly' – that's the launderer's verb in the Old Testament. Wash me deeply, pursue every last remainder of dirt in the fibres of my being, launder me. Notice the three words in verse 2: 'wipe away my transgression', 'wash me thoroughly from my iniquity', 'cleanse me from my sin'. Transgression, iniquity, sin. The dreadful thing about this passage is that it leaves nothing unsaid. When it looks at the state in which we find ourselves – transgression, iniquity, sin. When it looks at our needs as

God discerns them – wipe away, wash thoroughly, cleanse. What a picture of our nature and our behaviour and our needs lies behind those six words! There is no point at which we should say tonight, 'I'm not like that.' When a specialist is called in and makes a diagnosis he's not starting a debate, he's stopping a conversation. The Bible doesn't invite us to debate how we would react to this diagnosis, to say whether we feel like that or not and consent to it in our hearts. We sit before the diagnostic word of God and we learn what it is that we are like and how it is with us, irrespective of what we might feel or think or say about ourselves. Nothing is left unsaid.

But the marvellous thing about the passage is that when it looks at the Lord God, it doesn't leave anything unsaid either. In this psalm we are invited to see the God who sees. He sees what we are and He makes no secret of that which He finds; but He invites us to see Him who is seeing us, and the marvel is that He leaves nothing unsaid.

Here is what He is. Verse 1 '. . . according to thy lovingkindness, according to the multitude of thy tender mercies.' That's what He is like. He's a God of mercy, of lovingkindness. Not in general, and not in relation to somebody else, but in relation to *us* as the Scripture has diagnosed our state; in relation to sinners. And look what we may expect Him to do, as we see it through David's prayer. As His mercy and compassion reach out to us there is a wiping of the slate clean. Then there is a thorough washing. Then there is a cleansing. This is what He does.

And when we examine the passage further, we are told what He accomplishes through what He does. Do you see the order? Out of what He is, there springs what He does. Out of what He does, there springs what it is that He accomplishes for us. And so it is in verse 7: 'Purge me with hyssop and I shall be clean. Wash me, and I shall be whiter than snow. Again, in verse 9: 'Hide thy face from my sins and blot out all my iniquities.'

It is a marvellous word which opens verse 7. The word

'purge' is the translation which lies before me. We would
have to make up a word in English to be the exact
equivalent of that in the Hebrew. What word means 'to
take away contamination'? We say, to 'decontaminate'.
Here is the word which means to 'de-sin'. Take me, Lord,
in all that you know to be true about me; transgressions,
iniquities, sins. Take me and wipe the slate clean and wash
me and cleanse me thoroughly until in your great and
infinite mercy this is what you have accomplished for the
sinner. You have de-sinned him. 'Purge me with hyssop,
and I shall be clean.'

Let's gather those thoughts together under some
headings. Not really to add to them, perhaps just to
embroider a bit around them so that they may come home
with clarity.


### Sin

There is nothing about us that is untouched by sin. The
word 'sin' in verse two means a specific thing, the thing for
which when we come into the presence of God we would
have to say 'I'm sorry'. There is a lovely verse in the Bible
(Judges 20:16) speaking of the accurate slinging of stones.
And it says, concerning the expert slingers – who were also
left-handed men – that they could sling a stone at a
hairsbreadth and not miss. The word that is translated
there as 'miss' is of the same family of words as the one
here translated as 'sin'. Sin is a missing, a falling short of
the requirement of God, of the target He requires us to hit
smack in the centre.


### Iniquity

Go back to the beginning of verse 2. 'Iniquity' goes beyond
the specific sin to the nature from which it springs. It tells
us that we possess a flawed nature. The verb from which
the noun comes means to be bent or crooked. There is

something that is warped, at the heart of us; the flawed nature that lies behind the sinful act.

Brothers and sisters, if this were the whole of us, we would not be excused, but we would at least be in a position to try to make an excuse. 'I was born with a warped nature. In your diagnosis of me you have declared that I was in sin at the very moment I was conceived. Right back to the very earliest moment of the personal being and individual, sin was there. How could I avoid falling short and missing the mark in thought, and word, and deed and in everything else about me?' It would not be an excuse in biblical thinking, but we could at least make it.

## Rebellion

But the Word of God pounds us with yet a third word. In verse 1, the last word, 'wipe away my rebellions'. There is a wilfulness about the sinner. There is a candid weighing-up of the issues and a determination, over and over again, inwardly, outwardly, in personal behaviour, in relationships, you name it, we have done it. We have committed ourselves to a sinful state by wilful choice. There is nothing good about us, whether we view ourselves in the hidden man of the heart or whether we view ourselves most characteristically in the realm of choice or decision. There is nothing about us that is not touched by sin. But heed this, there is no aspect of sin beyond the reach of grace.

## Wash

At the beginning of verse 2 it says '*wash me* thoroughly'; and here you have your old-time launderer. Would you believe there was a time before detergents? A time when you could do marvels *without* the boil-wash? The launderer would take the laundry to running water, and pound it with his feet, hands and a stone, until he got right down into the fibres of the material and drove all the dirt out. There is no aspect of sin which is beyond the reach of grace! There is a work of God that reaches down into the hidden man of the heart; a launderer's work, a detergent work.

## Wipe

The end of verse 1 again: 'according to the multitude of your compassions, *wipe away.*' Oh, what a beautiful word. Here's washing-up to be done. Here's wiping away that which is outward, visible and observed about our sinfulness, the marks that God can see and the disfigurements others can see, caused by sin in our lives. There is no aspect of sin beyond the reach of grace!

## Cleanse

And again at the end of verse 2, '*cleanse me* from my sin.' It is a religious verb; it is a defilement that separates us from God. Here is a verb that says, remove the defilement that separates. Its main use as a verb is in the book of Leviticus, so you can see the significance of it. It is the sin-barrier between the sinner and God.

When we were in London at St Luke's Church, Hampstead, there was only one person that I know for certain was converted in the five years that we were there. And he wasn't converted at our church, he was converted at Westminster Chapel and then came to join us! He was a dear man. He came most beautifully and personally to the Lord. Then he found to his astonishment not only that he was still a sinner but that he could bring himself down into a pit of despair by falling into sins that he thought were gone.

We sat together and I brought him through the promises of God concerning the forgiveness of sin. Nothing would give him comfort, and nothing would lift him up, and nothing would convince him that he was not now lost for ever; until the Lord told me to stop talking to him in theory and start talking to him in pictures. 'Think of a blackboard,' I suggested to him. 'Think of the foulest word you have ever heard, written on that blackboard. Then think of somebody coming and wiping it away.'

Wash me thoroughly . . . wipe the slate clean . . . cleanse me. There is sin that is deep rooted in our nature, and grace can chase it. There is the sin which disfigures our lives and grace can wipe it away. There is the sin which separates between us and God, and grace can deal with it. There is no sin beyond the reach of grace. There is no change in the Lord when it comes to dealing with our sin. He is always and ever what He has always and ever been: He is a God of mercy and lovingkindness and of compassion.

## Mercy

The first reference in the Old Testament to the *mercy* of God is the same word that is used here; in connection with Noah, in Genesis 6:8. God has diagnosed the needs of the world and the plight of the sinner; He sees that man's iniquity is great. He repents that He has made man. He says, 'I'll destroy man.' But Noah found favour.

If you want to understand that, read it backwards. Favour found Noah. There was an outreaching of mercy to lay hold of one whom God determined to save.

## Lovingkindness

What a beautiful word that is! If you have a Revised Standard Version, it is probably translated 'steadfast love' – a beautiful translation and an accurate one. Psalm 100:5 says 'Your lovingkindness is for ever.' He changes not in His lovingkindness as He looks upon us in our sinful

state, and furthermore, He has a multitude of
compassions.

## Compassion

Do you remember when two girls stood before Solomon?
They were arguing as to which one was the mother of a
baby. One had lost her own baby and stolen the living
child from the other, and they stood before the king,
each saying 'It's mine.' So they argued until the king
could stand it no longer, and with that marvellous
wisdom which God gave him, he said 'Right, if you
cannot decide whose the child is, then give me a sword —
you can each have half.'

It says concerning the girl who was the mother of the
child, that her compassions were in *turmoil*. Do you feel
the force of that word now? It is full of emotion, it is full
of strong prevailing feeling.

The Bible allows us to think of God in most gloriously
human terms, as though, just like us, He had a mind,
emotions and a will. The word 'mercy' tells us that His
will is set upon our good, as sinners, and His forgiveness.
His mind says the word 'steadfast love', His mind is set
inflexibly on bringing us back to Himself, and His
emotions are engaged in a longing, passionate love for
us.

There is no sin of which we repent that will not be
forgiven. More than anything else, that is what Psalm 51
is about. David had fallen into the double sin of adultery
and murder, and search the law of God as he might, he
was met with a blank silence. There is no sacrifice
provided. There is no recourse to shed blood to cover the
sin of adultery and murder. There is a silence in the
sacrificial code, and this is the very core of the plight of
the sinner. Nothing can undo what has been done.
Nothing can make amends for it. Yet David comes to the
Lord, and he says, in verse 7, 'Purge me with hyssop.'

## Purge

Away back in Egypt, in Exodus 12, there was a people under the wrath of God. He came into the land of Egypt in judgement. And because in wrath He would remember mercy, and because He had covenanted to take a people for Himself, He said to the Israelites in the land of Egypt, 'Take a lamb and kill it. Take hyssop, and sprinkle blood around the door; and go in and stay.'

*There* is blood which can settle matters as between the sinner and God. 'I do not know,' says David, 'where that blood is, but you do.'

In the old code of the people of God, hyssop was used in the cleansing of a leper, and the leper himself was sprinkled with a mixture of blood and fresh water. *There* is blood which reaches subjectively into the sinner and deals with sin at the personal level where it has been committed. 'Purge me with hyssop.' What a leap into reality for David! 'Deep as the need, deep runs the blood, by heavenly hyssop well applied – unknown to me, but known to thee.'

A Lamb of God has died. And we know the name of the Lamb. It is a glad acceptance of a great reality. One sacrifice for sins, for ever; the blood of Jesus Christ His Son which cleanses and goes on cleansing us from all sin.

> And there, beneath its shadow,
> But on the further side,
> The darkness of an awful grave
> That gapes both deep and wide;
> And there between us stands the cross,
> Two arms outstretched to save,
> Like a watchman set to guard the way
> To that eternal grave.

How do we have access to that saving cross? Psalm 51:3 – 'I acknowledge my transgression'. The cross stands between us and the eternal judgement of God. Between us and the saving merits of the cross is the reality of personal acknowledgement and repentance.

'I acknowledge . . .' There is no sin of which we repent which will not be forgiven. 'I acknowledge . . .' Let us rejoice in what the Lord our God is. Let us rejoice in Him. Let us come to Him and say, 'I acknowledge my transgressions.' Amen.

# 'BE FILLED WITH THE SPIRIT'

*by Rev Harry Kilbride*

## Ephesians 5:18

There is quite a lot of talk today about being Spirit-filled, and not a little confusion. Sometimes I think we are beginning to divide the world into non-believers, believers, and Spirit-filled believers. I heard a sermon some time ago on tape where a person was predicting that the time would come when all Spirit-filled believers would be persecuted. He didn't seem to have a word for believers who were not Spirit-filled.

I wondered exactly who he had in mind for Spirit-filled believers. I have been asked by many people whether I am Spirit-filled, and when I have replied 'I hope so', or 'I want to be', I have noticed from their crest-fallen faces that they have already categorised me as non-Spirit-filled. And yet, I must be honest with you tonight here at Keswick, and say to you that there is something inside me – I am not quite sure what it is – but I am put off by people who claim to be Spirit-filled.

I have a feeling that if you were, you would be the last person to claim it. Rather, you would hope that by the grace of God, your heart and your life would be filled with the Spirit of God and of the Lord Jesus Christ, and by the way you live and by the way you behave and by your ministry to others and to the world, it would show. It is for the world to decide if those marks of fullness are upon our lives.

And yet we should want to be filled. There is such a thing as a Spirit-filled believer. The apostle Paul says 'be filled with the Spirit' – it is a command, and a passive one: 'Let yourself be filled' – God wants to do it. It is continuous – 'keep on letting yourself be filled' – it is for every day. And then – 'All of you' – it is plural. This is not just for some of the Ephesian believers and not for others.

Now we want to understand this statement, and to do so brings us into the biblical doctrine of the Holy Spirit, the Third Person of the Trinity. If we really want to understand something in Scripture that may be causing some difficulties, we have to follow certain rules, and one of them is to consider the whole of the Bible's teaching on that subject, not just one verse or passage; so that we get it in a balanced perspective. Another rule is to read the book in which the statement that we are considering is found, so that we understand the way the writer uses phrases and put it into its 'book context'; and then to look at the verses immediately around the statement to put it into its immediate context; and then we shall more likely save ourselves from error.

Well, we obviously cannot take a look at the Bible's entire teaching on the doctrine of the Holy Spirit tonight, but I will say something. I sometimes think that one of the mistakes we make is to make 'either-ors' of things that are 'both-ands'. The Holy Spirit is given for more than one reason.

For example, as I study the Bible I believe that the Lord Jesus Christ has given us the Holy Spirit *so that we might have the presence of Jesus in our hearts*. You will find that emphasised in our Lord's own teaching in John's Gospel chapters 14, 15 and 16, where He is telling the disciples that though He has to go away from them in body, He will not leave them desolate; He will come to them, His other self, the Comforter, the Paraclete, the Holy Spirit, will be with them and in them. So, when a person speaks about receiving the Lord Jesus Christ into their heart they mean that they have received the gift of the Holy Spirit. They have become a Christian, and Jesus' other self has been given to them in their hearts to abide.

A second reason why the Holy Spirit has been given, my Bible tells me, is *so that we might have the power of Jesus in our witness to the world*. Acts 1:8, 'You will receive power,' says the Lord Jesus, 'when the Holy Spirit comes upon you, and you shall be witnesses . . . But you cannot do it without power. The Holy Spirit is going to come and is going to give you power to witness for me and unto me to the whole world.'

A third reason, I believe, is *so that we might contribute to the ministry of Jesus for His body*. His body is the church, and He is busy building it up, and He does so by the Spirit within our hearts and lives, and believers within that body ministering to each other with spiritual gifts. The gifts we read about in (for example) Romans 12, 1 Corinthians 12-14, or Ephesians 4, are ministry gifts – they are not for self-adornment. They are to build up the body of Christ. If I am given an electric drill as a present, I would look silly wearing it round my neck like a tie. It is to *use*, for the benefit perhaps of myself, and of others.

The Lord Jesus has given gifts to His church. Nobody has all the gifts, nobody has no gift, so that we might be joined together in His body and build one another up. They are not for self-aggrandisement, they are for ministry to one another, and we want the fullness of the Spirit in that ministry.

Then I believe fourthly that He has given us His Spirit *so that we might have the character of Jesus in our lives*. He is called the *Holy* Spirit, and that is Scripture's favourite title for the Third Person of the Trinity, used over a hundred times. He wants – this is very important – to make us holy. What is the use of claiming to have Jesus in our hearts, if we do not live like Him, if we have no fruit of the Spirit in our lives? What is the use of having power to witness for Jesus, if the way we live and behave in the world is a denial of what we are claiming? What is the use of having gifts to use in the church if we are so ungodly and un-Christlike that we use them destructively rather than constructively? You could use an electric drill to build things, but you could probably use it to harm people and to do wrong things if you were a bad man – so it is with gifts.

Now, Ephesians 5 is in this fourth section. It speaks of how we live, and in Ephesians Paul often uses contrasts. What we were, and what we now are in Christ. How we used to behave, and the way we behave now, praise God! by grace. The way we used to behave and the way we ought to behave now if we are following the Lord Jesus Christ – and, I believe, here is a contrast. Verse 18: 'Do not get drunk on wine which leads to debauchery. Instead be filled with the Spirit.'

There is something which should *not* control you, he says. There is someone who *should* control you. People talk about 'being under the influence' of alcohol. Don't let alcohol control you, says Paul. Be under the control of the Spirit; be filled with the Spirit; let the Spirit control you.

He is contrasting two states, not (as some have mistakenly deduced from this text) comparing them as if similar. 'Observe a drunken person under the influence of drink,' some say; 'See how he behaves. Well, you behave the same way, only let it be the Holy Spirit rather than bottled spirit – but the behaviour will be similar.' No. I believe he is contrasting the two states. Let's look at this together just by going through the six marks, in the context in which he puts the statement. Let Scripture explain itself! Let the writer of verse 18 explain what he means by explaining 15-21. How will you live? How will you behave, if you are filled with the Spirit?

## Be careful how you live

Verse 15 contains the first mark. 'Be very careful how you live, not as unwise but wise'. In the original that is, '. . . how you walk'. I believe that that is significant; it is a biblical word for the Christian life, and has implications that we cannot go into tonight, such as steady progress, going somewhere, and so on. Seven times in Ephesians, Paul talks of the Christian life as 'walking'. 'Walk circumspectly,' he urges, in the King James translation. Isn't that the opposite of the way a drunken man walks? Being circumspect, being careful is exactly what he cannot do. Before the days of 'breathalysers', the police, I am told, used to ask anyone who was thought to be under the influence of drink to walk along a straight line painted on the floor. A drunkard would stagger about; he could not walk the line. But, the apostle Paul says, it is not like that when you are under the control of the Spirit. You look carefully how you walk, you walk circumspectly. It is like a person walking on a mountain path.

I do not believe God wants us to be anxious all the time, and yet neither does He want us to live carelessly. He wants us to be careful. This is a Spirit-filled life; a person who is Spirit-filled will scrutinise every area of his life, so that he might walk the narrow way carefully, knowing that sometimes it is a narrow walk, that Satan sometimes does seek to turn the signposts round, leave traps and try to make us fall. Be careful, then, how you live.

## Redeem the time

Verse 16: 'Making the most' (NIV) 'of every opportunity, because the days are evil.' That is rather a free translation. I don't know what your version has if you have another version than the New International Version, but it may say 'redeeming the time'. The Spirit-filled person redeems, buys back, the time. The world talks about 'spending time'. The Christian, evidently, is to talk of redeeming the time, because he cannot get enough of it, he has not got enough time to do all the things that he wants to do; and all the things that have to be done in the world. He cannot afford to waste time.

Isn't it true of a drunken man, that he wastes time? You wouldn't think of a person who is drunk, under the control of alcohol, as somebody spending time profitably; rather, in a profligate way, he wastes time. Indeed, this is what Paul says in verse 18. 'Do not get drunk with wine which leads to debauchery.' Wastefulness. You are to redeem the time.

I used to wonder how a Christian could buy back time. Once it's gone, it's gone. Well of course, that's true, but I went in 1977 to Palestine for the first time, and I saw what the Israelis had done to buy back the land. A million acres of land which had been otherwise useless had been reclaimed. One hundred thousand acres of marsh land and swamp had been drained, by hard sweat and years of labour; and then cultivated, terraced, sown and was now fruitful. Hillsides had had stones painstakingly removed so that vineyards and orchards could be planted, and the National Water Scheme had taken, and is taking, water from Galilee down to the South to the desert, to make it bloom with fruitfulness; redeeming the land. If you let land alone and do nothing with it it will go to waste; and I tell you, and I tell my own heart, if you do not work at this and we just leave time alone, it will tend to go to waste. Do you watch television? How much? In my first pastorate we had a Christmas party every year, and the first time I went to it I was amazed that every game the organisers had arranged was based on television programmes. I seemed to be the only person who had never heard of the programmes. They said to me, 'Pastor, haven't you seen the Generation Game?' I said 'No' — and we had a television; I'm not against it as a medium and I'm not against people enjoying themselves. But I came to the conclusion that my flock was watching a good deal too much of it. The longer I was there the more I got stewed up about it until honestly, if I'd felt I had authority from the Lord to do it, I would have gone round to every home and put a hammer – or an electric drill! – through the screen of the television. Because when it came to asking people to do something for the church – 'I haven't got time'; yet they could sit in front of that goggle-box night after night, that chewing-gum for the eyes, as I heard one preacher call it; wasting time.

Young people can waste it drinking coffee and talking about nothing; some students I've known do that. They call it 'having fellowship', but they're just wasting time, and one of the marks of the Spirit-filled Christian is that he wants to redeem the time and not to waste it. I am told that somebody put an advertisement in the 'lost and found' column of the newspapers: 'LOST: one golden hour, studied with sixty diamond minutes – irreplaceable.' How many golden bracelets have you lost recently?

## Want to know God's will

Verse 17: 'Therefore do not be foolish, but understand what the Lord's will is.' The Spirit-filled believer is a student, a disciple, he wants to know what God has for him and wants him to do. Where is he to find God's will? In the book, my friends, in the book. 'Thy Word is a lamp unto my feet and a light unto my path.'

'Let the Word of Christ dwell in you richly,' says Paul to the Colossians in the parallel passage in Colossians 3:16. To be filled with the Spirit is to have an appetite for the Word of God, to know what it is and to understand it. Get it right; get it in its balance; and have it rightly interpreted. Do you sit under a biblical ministry? I am amazed at the self-assurance of some Christians who think they can walk right and understand what the will of the Lord is, while sitting under an unbelieving ministry, the minister peddling poison and unbelief continually into their minds. I don't care what your denomination is, but I do care that you sit under a biblical ministry, because Christ has given some to be pastors and ministers to teach you and to teach me His Word, that we might know the will of God in every situation.

All Scripture is given by inspiration of God and is profitable for teaching, for rebuke, for training and for correction. Let's get into it. Let's be Bible Christians and know the Word. It is said of Samuel Rutherford, that great seventeenth-century Scots pastor and theologian, that he had his heart in heaven, his hands on the plough, and his feet walking in the ways of God. That's a Spirit-filled man.

### Speak to one another with psalms, hymns and spiritual songs. Sing and make music in your heart to the Lord

The Spirit-filled man, fourthly, sings a new song. We have a song that even angels cannot sing. We have been redeemed; we have been washed in the blood of the crucified one; we of all people ought to be ready to sing, and I know that here we are. We have something to sing about!

Notice the variety of things that we sing – psalms, hymns and spiritual songs. I am not sure of the difference. Some have suggested that they are Scriptures, doctrine and songs of Christian experience; well, you will certainly find all three in any good hymn book. Don't be tied to one type of singing. God has given us variety. Don't be snobbish in your musical tastes, will you? You know, there are some who are newly converted, or are young, and some of us who are neither, who do not always understand the wonderful poetry of the great hymns. Whereas, a simple chorus we can understand, and we can sing it as Paul says he wanted to sing it; with the Spirit and with his understanding. That is what we do when we sing with the Spirit. It is singing with the understanding, making melody to the Lord from the heart, and it is speaking to one another. Do you notice, there is a horizontal aspect? 'Speak to one another.' Don't be selfish, don't say 'I don't like that tune,' or, 'That's not my favourite hymn,' or 'I'm too tired to sing.' You will not say that if you are controlled by the Holy Spirit at that point, because you're singing for the benefit of other people, that they might be uplifted, that their hearts might be warmed, that the fire of God's Spirit in them might be kindled into a flame. And never, please, regard singing as a non-spiritual activity. I hate the word 'preliminaries'! A man in a church meeting once called the singing 'padding', and suggested we cut it out. I needed a spirit of self-control not to go and throttle him! He had never understood this passage.

I have time to mention only briefly two more things—

### Always give thanks to God the Father for everything

The fifth mark of a Spirit-filled Christian is (verse 20) that he or she is thankful. When? 'Always'. What for? 'Everything'. Yes, we give thanks for everything in the name of our Lord Jesus Christ, because we want to glorify Him even in our afflictions and our hurtful things. It does not mean that we necessarily like them, but there is a deeper level where the Spirit is witnessing with our spirit. We are saying, 'Lord Jesus, through my affliction let me glorify your name.' Notice how Paul gives Him His full title. So many today just seem to call Him 'Jesus'. Well, it is a precious name, but it is the Father's pleasure that we should call Him Lord, who from the beginning was the Mighty One, the Lord Jesus Christ.

### Submit to one another out of reverence for Christ

Verse 21 — you see the drunken person is often self-assertive, bragging, loud, boastful, touchy. You have to be careful not to annoy a drunk or he becomes fighting mad.

But Paul contrasts that with the person whose heart is under the control of the Holy Spirit. He said, 'submit'. 'Let this mind be in you which was in Christ Jesus.' Christ Jesus who, says John in chapter 13 of his Gospel, knowing that all things had been put under His feet, that He had come from God and was going to God, rose and took a towel, girded Himself, and washed the feet of His disciples.

Yes, we do need to be controlled by the Holy Spirit. We do need to be Spirit-filled believers. Paul says: 'Keep on – continually – letting yourselves – be filled with the Holy Spirit.' When we pray that prayer every morning (as we should) and open our hearts to that fullness as we want to, let's be sure that we know what will be the marks of the fullness when it comes.

# HOW ARE WE TO BE FILLED?

## by Rev George Duncan

*This address followed that of the Rev Harry Kilbride,
which precedes it in the present volume.*

## Philippians 2:12, 13

How important it is that we should note what Mr Kilbride
stressed, that 'being continually filled with the Holy
Spirit' is something which is commanded and recorded in
Scripture, but never claimed by anyone. We have had set
out for us the marks of what it means to be continually
filled with the Spirit, and we come now to the question,
'How?'

'Work out your own salvation with fear and trembling,
for God is at work in you both to will and to do of His
good pleasure.' It is one of the great texts of the Bible. Of
course Paul is not contradicting himself; it's not salvation
in the sense of getting back to God. He says, 'By the
works of the flesh shall no man be justified. I believe we
could render our text a little more freely: 'Work out your
own experience of God's saving grace. Work it out to its
completeness, with fear and trembling, for God is at work
in you both to will and to do of His good pleasure.' I
want, if I may, to share with you three aspects of the
Christian experience, lived out in that full sense, that
seem to me to be of very great importance and needing to
be stressed.

First of all we have to take into account

**The variations in our lives and the purposes of God**

Now it may be that what Paul is saying is, 'Now that I'm not visibly with you, work it all out on your own.' It may be that he's thinking more specifically and individually and saying to the Philippians, 'Work out your own experience of God's saving grace with fear and trembling.' In other words, the pattern of God's purpose for your life and mine is not necessarily intended to be the same; but there is infinite variety in God's working out, in the fullest sense, our experience of His saving grace.

It's been very well said that God never makes a duplicate, always an original. He does not want 'copy-cat Christians'. Even identical twins are not identical. I actually married one. I sometimes wonder whether it was the right one that turned up! They were so alike it was very difficult to tell them apart – but they were not identical. I wonder if the words of a saintly old Scottish minister, Fraser of Breo, would ring a bell in somebody's mind? He put it like this. 'My soul is not to hang at any man's girdle.' A lot of Christians today would do well to take that to heart. We're almost in danger of becoming a Corinthian church today, and human leadership is beginning to take over from the control of the Spirit.

I want to suggest that these variations in our lives and the purposes of God bring *encouragement for our hearts*. So often we face two kinds of dangers in growing up into Christian maturity. The first is the temptation to think we must be like some other Christian. I'm sure we are meant to learn from other Christians, but I don't find in my Bible that we're necessarily to try and be like them! You can sometimes see this more visibly in Christians holding prominent positions. I hold Billy Graham in the highest possible regard – he's done a wonderful work. But you know, after a visit from Billy Graham we get a whole crop of imitation Billy Grahams – men who develop a slight American accent, and twist their Bibles the way Billy twists his when he's preaching! That's a lot of nonsense. God only made one Billy, and He doesn't want any more. He made you to be you, because He wanted you to be you, not like anybody else.

I find among a lot of Free Church men a tendency to mould their ministry on that of Dr Martin Lloyd-Jones. The Doctor would preach for an hour, so they reckon they should preach for an hour. I tell them, 'If Dr Martin Lloyd-Jones did it, it would be unforgettable – if you do it, it will be unforgiveable!' And you and I are tempted, especially when we're young; we look at other Christians, and say 'I could never be that . . . I could never do that . . .' Well, perhaps the Lord never wants you to.

The other temptation is of course to try to make other people like us, to force them into our mould. I met an old lady who'd been carrying a great burden for years: somebody who claimed to have received the gift of speaking in tongues had told this poor soul that if she couldn't speak in tongues she wasn't a Christian. Well, that's a lot of nonsense! I believe in the gift of tongues; I don't think it's an important one, but I do think it is one of the gifts – but I don't think we're to tell anybody what gift they should have. That would be to arrogate to myself a power and authority that belongs to the Holy Spirit, not to me.

God wants each one of us to be different. He's put us at the centre of what Dr Paul Rees calls 'an expanding circle of contacts', and that's your area of opportunity. He has given you a personality that is unique, there's nobody else, because He wants to use it. God can reach people through your personality that He could never reach through mine.

So there's encouragement here for our hearts, and also of course there's *enrichment for the church*. That's why Paul points out, in 1 Corinthians 12, that every Christian has a gift and the Holy Spirit gives different gifts to different people, because different gifts are needed in the work of the church. He says, 'How ridiculous, if the whole body were to be all made up of one gift! Just a huge nose! Or just a huge foot walking along!' That is what Paul said, and I think he had a twinkle in his eye. And yet there are some people who seem to say that every Christian ought to have the same gift! May I submit, that's all a lot of nonsense.

Maybe you're a very good listener. You're no good at talking, but you're a good listener – well, I tell you, the world needs folk who listen just as much as it needs folk who talk. You might be no use at all in making a sermon, but you're very good at baking scones. God can use scones! Do you look upon your home as somewhere where you can show God's caring love to people and invite them in; not to talk to them about their soul, but just to show God's caring concern and love for them as people? There is a variation in our lives and the purposes of God. We've got to be ready and willing to accept ourselves. I wonder whether somebody needs to do that, to accept the fact that you are different? Maybe you're not married. Prepare to accept that until God changes it, because there are things you can do that married people can't.

Encouragement for our hearts, enrichment for the church, and then to the main thrust – 'for God is at work in you.'

## The operation in our lives of the Spirit of God

'God is at work *in you*.' But is He? Is He? And I want to probe behind that very searching message of Mr Kilbride's that we've been listening to: the mark of the life that is continually being filled with the Spirit as its source. But how?

I want to note first of all, *how the Holy Spirit can be restrained in our lives*. My Bible makes it quite clear. I know many people make much of 'irresistible grace', but it's not a phrase I find anywhere in my Bible, nor do I find anywhere that God's grace is irresistible either to sinners or saints. As for sinners, I find Jesus grieving over Jerusalem, and Stephen challenging his accusers, 'You do always resist the Spirit of God' – nothing irresistible there! As for believers, I find Paul warning the believers, 'Grieve not the Holy Spirit.' I can grieve Him! I find Paul saying 'Quench not the Spirit.' I can quench Him! He says to Timothy, 'Neglect not the Spirit' – so I can neglect the gift, the Holy Spirit. There's nothing irresistible there. And I believe that the tragedy in the church today is that the Holy Spirit is restrained, grieved, quenched, neglected. So if I want to consider how the Holy Spirit can be restrained in my life I have to consider how He may be released in my life. He's not to be a prisoner.

I remember a very godly Scottish minister saying that the answer to the question, 'How do you grieve the Holy Spirit?' was this. We grieve the Holy Spirit when we fail to allow Him in us to do that for which He has been given. We're thinking of the operation of the Holy Spirit in our lives. There's a simple three-fold distinction which I think we need to get hold of if we're not going to get confused.

First, there's *the life the Holy Spirit wants to live in me*. That's obvious – He's a person. It's a divine life. He's God! Both love and life and that character of the divine Spirit will determine the life He wants to live. That means there'll be a whole lot of things He'll want out, a whole lot of things He'll want to bring in; but there is a life He wants to live. I've got to let Him live that life.

Then of course there's *the gift He wants to give*. Our Bible makes that plain: 1 Corinthians 12; Ephesians 4; Romans 12; we've heard about that. But we need to remember the diversity of the gifts and the sovereignty of the giver. Never, never, never, never, never tell anybody they ought to have any gift. It's quite wrong. And be very careful about claiming a gift. Some people claim the gift of being preachers, but the congregation disagree when they hear the man preach! No. You don't claim gifts – usually, the church sees them.

Then there's something else; there are *things He wants to do in me*. We call these the ministries of the Holy Spirit. And if you were to ask me, what is the secret of the power of the Holy Spirit, I would submit that it's nothing to do with the gifts. I can have the gift without the power. I can have the gift of preaching without the power of the Spirit quite easily, but if the Holy Spirit is not being allowed to do in me the things He's been given to do, then the power has gone. If I'm not allowing Him to live the life He wants to live, the power's gone, because I'm grieving Him. And you know, there's one very important question that every Christian ought to ask – what does the Holy Spirit want to do in my life? What has He been given to do? Have you ever asked that question? Because there are things the Holy Spirit has been given to do.

I can only name them, we haven't got time to go into them in detail. The difference between a gift and a ministry of the Spirit is that the gift is used occasionally and gifts differ from Christian to Christian. The ministries are the things in almost continual use, far more frequently than the gifts. And there are things that the Holy Spirit wants to do in every Christian.

He wants *to teach us*. Jesus spoke about that. John 14:26, 16:30. 'He will teach you.' Do you give Him the opportunity? The importance of spending time with your Bible is not to conform to a pattern of evangelical piety, it's in order that the Holy Spirit can teach you.

He's been given *to seal your life*. Paul says, 'When you believed, you were sealed with the Holy Spirit.' Dr Jowett says that 'seal' primarily indicates ownership.

One of the things the Holy Spirit wants to do in your life is to *bring everything under the authority of Jesus Christ*. That's one of the things He's been given to do.

*The praying ministry* – Romans 8:26 – we don't know how or what to pray. He's been given to help us in private prayer, in corporate prayer. How much time do we give to that?

*The caring ministry* – we've lost sight of this! 'The love of God,' says Paul, 'has been shed abroad in our hearts by the Holy Spirit given to us.' That's not a gift of the Spirit – it's part of His very nature. He wants to care for others, and this, of course, is where a lot of our thinking about Christian love is sloppy and shallow. The biblical word 'agapé' is very little used in classical Greek, and it means something infinitely precious, quite different from the word for physical love. It's a different dimension altogether.

The caring ministry means that people matter. How many people really matter to you? A girl once said to me in one of my churches, 'The trouble with you people is that you're only interested in my soul. You want to see me converted.' Of course we did, but the trouble was that that was all we were interested in. We weren't interested in her as a person, but God was.

*The leading ministry* – 'as many as are led by the Spirit of Christ'. There's lots going on today that makes me think of Dr Paul Rees's phrase about Christians wanting to be 'big ducks in small puddles'. A leadership craze!

And what about *the testifying ministry*? 'He shall testify to me.' I used to think that that meant that the Holy Spirit would testify to me about Christ, and I was right and I was wrong. God not only wants to testify *to* me, He wants to testify *through* me. That means I've got to be ready to open my lips and my mouth. When did you last say a word for Jesus to anybody?

Well, there it is. The Holy Spirit can be restrained, the Holy Spirit must be released. We've thought of the variations in our lives and the purposes of God, the operation in our lives of the Spirit of God; finally and very briefly,

## The motivation in our lives of the fear of God

I want if I may in closing to bring in a slight counter-balance to something which has been said here and with which I absolutely agree. We're getting far too familiar with God. But what kind of fear are we talking about? The fear of a tyrant, or the fear of a father of whose love we are so sure?

I love the story of Dr Barnhouse, that most dogmatic of all Presbyterian American preachers to preach from this platform. He once asked a Roman Catholic priest, 'One thing bothers me; that's the place you give to Mary the mother of our Lord. Why do you do it?'

The Roman Catholic priest thought for a moment and then said, 'If I were going to meet the King, I would like somebody to introduce me.'

'But not,' replied Dr Barnhouse, 'if the King was your father.'


It's love's fear. There is a failure that love dreads. When I played cricket when I was young, I was always scared when I saw my father among the spectators. I wasn't afraid of the bowler. I was afraid of disappointing Dad.

I think it was William Barclay who said that the highest motivation is to see the light in someone's eyes. If you're a Mum or a Dad and you go to a school concert, you see your child in the choir looking this way and that; and then they see you, and they're content. They're not just there to sing as part of the choir. They're there to sing because you're there, and they want to give you delight.

I love that young people's hymn,

> Just as I am, young, strong and free
> To be the best that I can be,
> For truth, and righteousness, and thee
> Lord of my life – I come.

The verse I love best is this:

> And for thy sake to win renown,
> And then to take the victor's crown,
> And at thy feet to lay it down,
> Lord of my life – I come.

I don't want to raise a great congregation like this to an emotional 'high'. I'm not interested in that kind of spiritual 'high'. There's a lot of it around today! I want us to get down to the nitty-gritty of how to be continually being filled with the Spirit. It's something I've got to watch very carefully every day of my life; and if I'm letting Him do what He's been given to do, I shall find that I am being filled. Maybe I won't notice it; but others will, and God will, and He'll start using me. Are you, am I, being filled? If that's what it means, these are the marks, this is the secret! Nothing very exciting, a bit down-to-earth, but that's what being a Christian, being filled with the Spirit, is all about.

Are we willing for the nitty-gritty business? Or do we just want the spiritual 'high'?

# THE PRODIGAL SON

## by Dr Ronald Dunn

## Luke 15:11-24

I've always felt that one of the great tragedies in life is for a person not to believe in God. It is beyond my comprehension that anyone could say 'There is no God.' But I have come to believe that there is something even more tragic than not believing in God, and that is, believing in the wrong kind of God. I think it may be easier to win a man to faith in Christ who originally does not even believe in God, than to win a man who does believe in God but the wrong kind of God. I think Jesus had an easier time with the publicans and sinners than with the Pharisees and Sadducees. It's terrible to be lost, but it's worse to be lost in religion, and that's why all through the Scriptures you have this emphasis repeated again and again, that Jesus came to reveal the Father. Why should that be necessary? Because man himself, by his own ingenuity and with his own cleverness, cannot know what kind of God it is we serve and worship. Jesus came to make the invisible visible, the unapproachable approachable. He came to make the inaccessible God accessible, and He opened our eyes when He said, 'He that hath seen me hath seen God.' The great heartbeat of the gospel is that man may know God.

But not just know that there is a God. It's not enough

just to believe that there is a God, that all of this vast universe did not simply happen, that there is a creative power behind it. It's not enough simply to believe that. It is imperative that we believe in the right kind of God. You and I do not worship God as He is; we worship Him as we conceive Him to be. Our worship of God is limited by our concept of God. If we have wrong ideas about God, our worship will be incorrect.

You remember in John 4, when Jesus talked to the woman of Samaria at Jacob's Well. After a while she revealed her ignorance by saying, 'We know that you folks believe there is one particular place you have to worship, that worship is limited by geographical locations.' Jesus tried to correct her. 'But', He said, 'they that worship God must worship Him in spirit and in truth.' Why? 'First of all,' He says, 'God is Spirit.' Do you see what Jesus is trying to do with this woman? He is saying, 'The reason you don't have the right idea of worship is that you don't have the right idea of God. He is Spirit. He's not limited by geographical locations. He is Spirit. We must worship Him according to His nature, in spirit and truth.' Our concept of God determines the way we worship Him.

Go to 1 John 1. 'God is light, and if we have fellowship in Him we must' – what? – 'Walk in the light as He is in the light.' Not only my worship but also my walk is determined by my concept of God. Why must I walk in the light? Because God is in the light, and whatever God is that's how I must be, because the Christian life is nothing more than my reaction to the nature and character of God. That's all the Christian life is. He is light, therefore I must walk in the light. We love Him. Why? Because He first loved us. Be ye holy. Why? Because He is holy. And all through the Scriptures, the important thing is that I should know what kind of God it is that I am worshipping. If my concept of God is defective then everything about my Christian living will be defective.

And that's why Luke 15 is important. What Jesus is

doing in this string of parables is revealing to us the kind of God it is that we worship.

The passage opens with the Pharisees criticising Jesus because He was eating with publicans, and He begins telling these parables. Why? He's saying, the trouble with you Pharisees is you don't know what kind of God it is you're talking about. So all these parables reveal to us the heavenly Father, and I want to look especially at the parable of the prodigal son – but you know, it is actually a parable about the father. It's a picture not of a runaway boy – he's only incidental to the story – rather, it is a picture of the heart of the father. What Jesus is doing is throwing aside the curtains and giving us a glimpse into the very heart of God Himself.

What kind of God is it we worship? First of all, Jesus points out to us,

## He is a God who grieves

He has the capacity to grieve over every prodigal child of His that runs away.

For years as I read this story I felt so sorry for that boy. I followed him round, I wanted to try to help him – 'Hang on to a bit of that, boy, you're going to need that one of these days; don't spend it like that!' And after a while he's spent it and nobody helps him. All his friends have suddenly disappeared, and bless his heart, pity the poor boy, he winds up in a pig bin feeding pigs. And you know, I always felt sorry for him.

Until I became a father. Then I felt sorry for the father.

Because I want to ask you, who is it in this story that hurts the most? Who has the greatest capacity for hurt? It's the father. You see there's something both wonderful and un-wonderful about love. It makes you vulnerable to pain. It puts you at the mercy of hurt. And this boy is suffering, but his suffering is not to be compared with that of his father. I think it's one of the most remarkable things in all Scripture that when Jesus Christ came to reveal to us God, and when God said to Himself, I want to show man who I am, and how can I do that? – What word can I use, what relationship will describe how I feel about my creation? – that out of all the choices that God had He chose the word 'Father'. Jesus came and revealed to us that God is more than a God of might, wisdom, power and creative genius. He is first and foremost our Father. You'll never find anybody in the Old Testament calling God Father, not in the sense of Father of an individual. Abraham and David never called Him Father. But when Jesus came, He said, 'This is the way to pray. Say: Our Father.'

Have you noticed, that Scripture never speaks of God *becoming* our Father? It speaks of us becoming His children, but never vice-versa. There is a very real sense in which He has always been our Father, but we have not always been His children. In salvation, you see, it is not God who needs to be changed. It is we who need to be changed. He has always loved us as a Father. Jesus said, 'I want you to know that God is your Father. He is your Father, and a Father grieves.'

We have two children. We've had three. We lost one when he was eighteen but we have a son now who's twenty-one, getting ready to get married. Soon as we get back I'm performing the ceremony. There's a phrase in Galatians where Paul says, 'I travail again until Christ be formed in you.' And you know, I discovered that there is a pain in bringing a child into the world, but there is a further pain in bringing a child up into the world. I know something of that pain. I used to say, 'I'll be glad when they get grown up and married, and I won't have to worry about them any more.' Then a few years ago I met a minister in his early sixties. He was driving me back to my hotel and as he pulled up to let me out, he began to weep. He told me that he was a pastor, and that he desperately needed to talk to somebody. His thirty-nine-year old son, a doctor with a wife and children, was drinking, was involved with other women, and had lost his practice and his home. As he told me about his hurt I sat there and thought to myself, Dear Lord – do you mean to tell me that even when they're on their own, even when they're thirty-nine, the father still worries about the son? That's the most discouraging thought I've ever had in my life!

There'll never be a time, I realised then, when I'll be free from the hurt of my children. You're always the father. That's why Isaiah says of God, 'In all their afflictions, I am afflicted.' I think it's one of the most beautiful pictures in all the Scriptures.

When the young man came home, it says in verse 20, he arose and came to his father, but 'when he was yet a great way off, his father saw him.' I believe that that father, every day, stood by the window. Do you know what it means to stand in front of a window, looking as hard as you can and hoping that you will catch just a glimpse of a returning runaway? This is what Jesus says God is like. That's why it hurts me when people say, 'Well, my sin damages nobody but myself.' Oh yes, it does. It nailed Jesus to a cross, and it still inflicts pain into the heart of your heavenly Father.

But there is something else.

## He is a God who receives

He received us just as we are. You notice, there is no stinging word of rebuke from the father? I think that's one of the things I like best about him. One of my favourite verses is in James 1. He's talking about falling into various kind of trials, and he says that in the midst of those trials, 'if any man lack wisdom let him ask of God, who gives liberally to all men and upbraideth not.' That means He doesn't rebuke us for getting into the mess in the first place. When we come to God and say 'Lord, I'm in a mess and I need some wisdom to get out of it', He doesn't say 'Well, all right, but first I'm going to tell you something . . .'

I was once going through some trial. I didn't want advice, I didn't want a sermonette, I just wanted someone to pat me on the shoulder and say, 'There, there; God ought to be ashamed, the way He's treating you.' I was feeling sorry for myself and I wanted someone else to feel sorry for me too.

So I sought out one of my friends and unloaded my story. The only thing was, that this person had never had a day's trouble. He didn't know what heartbreak or trouble was. And when I got through telling him my story, you know what he said? He said, 'Ron, how in the world could you have been so stupid as to get yourself in a mess like that?'

If my heart was breaking and he was the only person on the face of the earth, I wouldn't go back to him. He couldn't give me help without first upbraiding me. But every time I come to the Lord and I say 'Lord, I've sinned again, and I know I've promised not to do this,' the Lord doesn't preach me a sermon before He forgives me. This Father receives us just as we are.

In dealing with this, let me point out something in the speech of this boy. In the prodigal's talk to himself, he said one thing right and two things wrong.

First of all, he wakes up. He comes to himself in that pig pen (verse 17). That's about the first and only thing he said right. Suddenly he said, 'My goodness – I'm a son. My father's hired servants are getting along better than I am.' Did you know, friends, that a child of God who is in the far country, out of fellowship with God, gets along worse in this world than the people who are lost? The devil is the prince of this world, and I tell you he sometimes takes better care of his own than he takes of the Lord's. A lost person can be happier in this world than a backsliding

Christian. That's the first thing he said, and he said it right.

But he said two other things, and missed by a mile; because he did not understand his father. That's why most boys run away in the first place. That's why most Christians find themselves in the far country. They don't understand the nature of their Father.

Two things. First, 'I will go to my father and I'll say to my father – I am no longer worthy to be called your son.' Every time I read that I want to yell at him; 'Where did you get the idea that you were worthy in the first place?' You see pride must have been one of this young man's problems. He must have felt at one time that he *was* worthy of being his father's son. Well, I have news for you, fellow; you never were worthy. You know something? Many a time I have sinned against God and made a mess of my life, and I've been reluctant to come back to the Lord because I've said to myself, I'm not worthy to come back to God, to pray, to preach, to serve the Lord. Friend, I have news for you . . . *you were never worthy in the first place.* And isn't it wonderful to know that my sin made me no less worthy than I ever was? God didn't love me in the first place because I was worthy of His love. He has never answered my prayers because I am worthy. My sins cannot make me any less worthy and my righteousness cannot make me any more worthy. You remember in Acts, when they healed the lame man and afterwards they were questioned. Peter said, 'We don't want you to misunderstand; this man was not healed by our power or our holiness.' We often get the idea that if we're living as we ought to live this gives us an extra inch with God and somehow increases our favour. Then when we find ourselves falling flat on our face and sinning against God, we're crushed and feel guilty and dirty. Why? Because we say, I'm no longer worthy. I have good news for you! You never were worthy! And God never did base His relationship with you on the fact that you were worthy. It's on the fact that Jesus is worthy.

His second mistake was, 'I will say to my father, make me as one of thy hired servants.' Why would he say that? He had such a mistaken view of his father, He thought that his sin would affect his father's love for him, that it would somehow not only change the son but change the father. In the story, the father interrupted him. Sin doesn't change the father. In the story, the father interrupted him. Sin doesn't change the way God thinks of me. This is the reason that sometimes we're mistaken because we create God in our own image, and when *we* discover people's sin, it affects the way we think about them. I've noticed time and time again as a pastor that when somebody has come to me and told me about some secret sin, it changes our relationship. Not on my part, but his. He's ashamed to look at me, and more often than not he eventually goes off and joins some other church where the pastor doesn't know his secret. You know why they do that? They think to themselves, now that the pastor knows what I'm really like, he'll never think of me as highly as he once did. That's the way we are, and the tragedy is, that's the way we think God is. But God has a fixed and established attitude of love and grace, and my sin doesn't cause Him to think a bit less of me. He says, 'Make me as one of thy hired servants.' The father says, 'No, I'll make you as my son.'

So Jesus is saying that that's the kind of God we have. First, He is a God who grieves over every one of us. Second, He is a God who receives us just as we are. Of course He doesn't let us stay as we are. He demands that the marks of the old country be taken off and covered with the marks of a returning child, but He receives us just as we are. The last word is this;

## He treats us as though we'd never been away

Notice verse 22. The father re-establishes the son into his former position of sonship.

The father does two things. Firstly he forgives; and then,

he just gives. Firstly, he welcomes this son. He goes out and smothers him with hugs and kisses and brings him back into the house. Then what? You know, this is the wonderful thing about our Lord. He always gives us more than we expect. The son was expecting to be treated like a slave. The father forgave him, but gave him more. He said, 'Put shoes on his feet' – which is the sign of sonship; 'put a ring on his finger' – which is the sign of authority; 'put a robe on his shoulders' – which is the sign of fellowship and abundance; 'and kill the fatted calf.' It was the best one. 'I'm not ashamed of this son – bring all your friends!'

You say, 'Oh, surely you want to keep it quiet – I mean aren't you ashamed that your boy has run off . . .?' He said, 'I'm not ashamed to be called their God. You call in all the friends, let's have a party and make merry.' He always gives us more than we expect.

I hear that thief as he hangs on the cross. He says, 'Lord, remember me when thou comest into thy kingdom.' He didn't have much theology, but what he was saying was, 'Lord, I know that someday, millenia from now, you'll have a kingdom. And when that happens, could you just remember me?' And Jesus says, 'I'll do a lot more than that. Today, not in a millenium, but today, you shall be with me; not just in remembrance, but in Paradise.'

To the woman at the well He says, 'Woman, let me give you a drink and I promise you you'll never thirst again.' He gives us always more than we expect. He treats us as though we'd never been away.

Maybe you've been away from the Father. It may be, you've never come to the Father in the first place. He may ba a Father but you're not a son to Him. Perhaps you've never had that experience of salvation in which, by definite will of your own, you have put your faith and trust in Jesus, and maybe you're reluctant to do so because you feel unworthy.

He's a Father. He grieves over you today. I promise you, He'll receive you just as you are now. You say 'I must change so many things first – I need to get ready to come.'

No, you come just as you are 'without one plea. For his blood was shed for thee.'

You may already be a son or daughter, but you're in the far country. How long does it take, to get to the far country? Oh, you're there in just a second. The far country is just a step away, just a disobedience away, and maybe you've fallen into sin and said to yourself 'I know that I can never be the same, I know I can never again have fellowship with God, I can never again know God's favour, I am no more worthy to be called your son.'

That's not true. You're just as worthy now as you ever were. He is a Father who is grieving over you today, and He'll receive you just as you are and He'll treat you as though you've never been away.

# STEPHEN – MAN OF CHARACTER

*by Rev Eric Alexander*

## Acts 6:5-8:3

As we draw to the close of the teaching ministry of this convention I want us to return to the point at which we began, and that means returning to the book of Acts and to the picture in chapters 6 and 7 of the church which made that high and holy resolve in 6:4[1], 'We will devote ourselves to prayer and to the ministry of the Word.' That church produced some remarkable men, and among them was Stephen the martyr, to whom I want to turn with you now.

Stephen, the first Christian leader to lay down his life for the gospel, dominates the whole of the passage from 6:5 to 8:3. Very significantly, his death introduces us to the figure who is going to dominate the rest of the book: 7:58, 'The witnesses laid down their clothes at the feet of a young man named Saul.' Saul was of course Saul of Tarsus, who became Paul the apostle to the gentiles.

We are told three things about Stephen in this passage. First,

### He was a man who reflected something of the character of God

I'm thinking of course of 6:15 – 'his face was like the face of an angel.' What that means is that in the most unselfconscious way Stephen's whole bearing and life and character had a glory and a beauty which could not be hidden.

You will notice that the word which Luke repeatedly uses to describe Stephen is the word 'fullness'; he uses it in 6:5, 6:8, and 7:55. These references add up to the simple fact that Stephen is a man who is just full of God and of the beauty and glory of the character of God as it is revealed in Jesus Christ. So if you want to know how you can recognise a life that is filled and dominated by the Holy Spirit, it is at a man such as Stephen that you should look. He is one of the most striking examples in the New Testament.

The marks of the fullness are very significant. At least five can be identified, and I want to ask you to look with me at them. As we look it will not take much imagination to see that what Luke is really describing for us from Stephen's character is the kind of moral glory which is the fruit of the Spirit.

The first of the marks is that *he possessed a manly godliness*. There is a remarkable strength of character about him. His angelic countenance does not mean weakness. In 6:9, 10 he towers above his detractors with a manliness and godliness that leaves them silent and sends them scurrying to find witnesses. That same godliness is seen in his steadfastness and perseverance in all kinds of circumstances, so that when they are gnashing their teeth and plotting his death he is more aware of the glory of God than the wrath of men. In 7:54, 55 it is the ministry of the Holy Spirit to produce this strong, stable persevering godliness in our character. It is this persevering steadfastness which is the mark of the man who is filled with all the fullness of God — not a man who streaks off into the atmosphere like a firework and comes down again like a damp squib. God knows how much we need that quality of character, produced by the Holy Spirit, in the modern church.

Secondly, *he possessed a godly wisdom*. I'm thinking especially of 6:10. They were overwhelmed by the profound wisdom Stephen showed as he spoke to these learned men. It was not the weight of his own learning; in fact it is not really an academic thing at all. It is the fulfilment of Jesus' promise in Luke 21:15, 'I will give you words and wisdom which none of your adversaries will be able to resist or contradict.' It is not the wisdom which comes from the university or the seminary. It comes with a growth in grace and godliness, with a life that is filled with all the fullness of God. It is possible for a man to be greatly gifted intellectually and yet be a baby in wisdom; and it is possible for another man to have very little intellectual training and yet in godly wisdom to be a giant.

This is one of the elements we desperately cry out to God for in the evangelical church in our day. What is the secret? I think it's to be found in places like Psalm 119. Listen to Psalm 119:97:

> O how I love your law! I meditate on it all day long. Your commandments make me wiser than my enemies, for they are ever with me. I have more insight than all my teachers, for I meditate on your statutes. I have more understanding than the elders, for I obey your precepts.

The fullness of the Holy Spirit also produces *a love of Scripture*. There is a connection with the foregoing. The most obvious conclusion one can draw about Stephen from the seventh chapter of Acts is that a man who is filled with the Holy Spirit is also filled with the Holy Scripture. It just pours out of Stephen, for his heart and mind were steeped in it. And this is a vital index to the character of the man.

May I press this especially upon young people who are here, whom God is shaping for the future? You to whom those of us who are older are looking, in these exciting and tremendously significant years of the last part of the twentieth century. I say to you, above all other things in the world that you concentrate on, give yourselves to an earnest, serious study of the Scriptures. There is nothing in the world so important. Nothing will form your character more than that, nothing shape you for the future more, nothing create a fruitful servant of God out of you more than that.

Not all are called to be scholars, but I want to say that every one of us is called to be a student of Holy Scripture. The apostles pressed this on us throughout the whole of their pastoral care for God's people. Pray for a new love of Scripture and a deeper appetite. And let me tell you that there is a French proverb which says 'The appetite grows with eating.'

The fullness of the Holy Spirit is also marked in Stephen's case by *a willingness to serve in ordinary and insignificant ways and places*. Recollect the background of Stephen in 6:3, and the problems in the early church which we were thinking about on Saturday evening[2]. Stephen was one of the deacons chosen to serve tables. How long he did it we don't know, but that was his first ministry. And God proved him there; and he proved God there. There is a lesson of vital importance here that we greatly need to learn. Christian character is most tested and trained in situations of obscurity and in tasks which might seem menial and distasteful.

One of the great problems in exercising our gifts is that so many people want to exercise them in the limelight. A minister friend was lamenting that while his congregation demanded tasks and responsibilities, he didn't notice any stampede to the kitchen to wash the dishes, or a queue to get the brush from the caretaker to help him sweep up; no crowds of people clamour to sit with the lonely widow in obscurity, who's had a stroke and can hardly speak.

But I know a young woman who became one of the most fruitful servants of God I know. And the first evidence of her godliness which struck people was that she was faithful in the ordinary and the distasteful and insignificant things.

Don't go away from Keswick seeking some exalted sphere of service, if you are not willing to spend your life washing your fellow-disciples' feet if that should be God's choice for you. Do I care for the glory of the Lord Jesus, or am I interested in a life that is going to exalt me? That is the issue.

Out of that let me mention the fifth thing that marked Stephen's life, and you will see the marks of the Lord Jesus on him there. *He had a selflessness which was ready to sacrifice everything for the glory of God.* And this is what made him like Jesus. His life is marked by self-denial and self-sacrifice; and it's all because his vision at the end of his life had been his vision throughout his life, and that was the glory of God.

Now these are the great hallmarks of Stephen as a man of God. May I just draw your attention to the church fellowship out of which such a character as Stephen's was produced and formed. It was a church which (6:4) had settled its priorities. Priorities are of vital importance within the life and ministry of the church in our own day. It is not that we are interested in establishing a certain pattern; it is that we are concerned about producing men and women of God whose lives will tell for Him in a needy world. And such men and women are born out of a church where the priorities are apostolic. I am disturbed to receive quantities of literature on church growth from various parts of the world when almost everything is concerned with church growth in numerical terms. Beloved, I do not think that God is greatly impressed with a church that is expanding numerically when it is not deepening spiritually. I don't think quantity matters to God so much as quality. We need these marks of the fullness which characterised Stephen, the man who reflected something of the character of God.

### He was a messenger who preached the whole counsel of God

Stephen's ministry is so important that the longest chapter in Acts (7) is devoted to it. The vital thing about the whole of Stephen's public ministry seems to have been that the power of

God was upon and in him. People felt it. There was a persuasive wisdom which had nothing to do with man but came from God. It was God the Holy Spirit filled him, reaching down into the conscience and bringing conviction. If you pray for your ministers that is what you should pray for. You ought to pray for the power of God in the pulpits of our land. Stephen was such a man who, as a messenger of God, preached the whole counsel of God.

You will notice that his whole address is just a prolonged exposition of Scripture. He draws a straight line from Abraham (7:2) right through to Christ (7:52). What he is doing is expounding the whole of the Word of God. And the power of the Spirit came down, blew like the wind upon the people, and brought conviction. That conviction burned either into contrition, repentance and faith, or into bitterness and hardness and unbelief. And it burned in that latter direction upon them. But oh, what an example Stephen's ministry is! It is the whole counsel of God from the whole Word of God. We need his example in our day. In Scotland, which is the only place I'm qualified to speak of, many students come out of theological colleges amazingly ignorant of great tracts of the Bible (and you need to pray about that, too).

### He was a martyr for the glory of God

I want to say something about his death, and then a closing word about its fruits.

There are clearly two sides to the fact of Stephen's death. On the one hand there is the wrath and hatred of the people, convicted by the Word and the Spirit of God together biting into their souls. That, I suppose, is the basic physical reason behind Stephen's death.

But there's another side to the fact of his death. 'Full of the Holy Spirit, Stephen gazed into heaven . . . and he said "Behold, I see the heavens opened, and the Son of Man standing at the right hand of God"' (7:55). Do you know,

I believe that was what concluded the matter for Stephen. I think it would have been impossible for him to come back and live in this world after that. He had caught a vision of the infinite glory; and his whole being was drawn out to what he saw, and I think it spoiled him for the earth for ever. And he cried, 'Lord Jesus, receive my spirit.'

That's the fact of Stephen's death, but we need to notice in closing, the fruit. Again, it's twofold. It's firstly the occasion for the outbreak of persecution led by Saul of Tarsus, whose conscience was clearly inflamed (8:3); and that persecution drove the church out of Jerusalem to Judea and Samaria. There's a sense in which Stephen's sermon drove them out theologically and biblically, and Saul's persecution drove them out physically and geographically. So the martyrdom of Stephen was, in a gracious sense in the purpose of God, bearing fruit already. It's significant that the word for 'witness' in the New Testament is the word from which we derive our word 'martyr'.

But the other fruit is even more significant. In 7:58 we read that the witnesses laid their clothes at the feet of a young man named Saul; and (8:1) 'Saul was there giving consent to his death.' I reckon Saul was at least within earshot of that Spirit-anointed ministry. I would guess that the Word of God had stabbed his conscience. However, Saul went away in a blind rage, to ravage the church of God. But even as he was on his way to reap destruction in the church at Damascus, the heavens opened a second time and the Lord Jesus spoke to Saul. And he fell down, blinded by that same glory that had drawn Stephen's soul out towards heaven.

In a profound sense Saul of Tarsus was a fruit of Stephen's death. Think of it. Some might have said his life was cut off prematurely. But the striking thing is that his life was the fuel which set alight such a flame for the glory of God in the ancient world that it has never had such a parallel. His life is going to be the seed from which there will grow something for the glory of God in the ancient world, in the life of this man Saul. My Christian brothers and sisters, we need to think desperately in these days of the generation that is coming behind us. We need a sense of history. We need to ask ourselves not only what is blessing ourselves, and what we want the Holy Spirit to do for us. We need to ask, what legacy are we leaving for the generation coming behind us?

Young people, you need to ask that too. You need to ask in terms of the character God is building into your life; what sort of children are you going to have? What spiritual progeny will you produce? So much will depend on this. It is the ultimate glory of Stephen's life that as he gladly offered himself up a living sacrifice to God, out of that there came the fruit of the apostle Paul.

I don't want to be melodramatic, but I think I would gladly give my very life if it were to produce somebody like Paul for the next generation – wouldn't you?

But there is a cost. Do you know these words of Jim Elliot?

> Saturate me with the oil of the Spirit so that I may be aflame. But flame is transient, often short-lived. Canst thou bear this, my sole, short life? But in me there dwells the Spirit of the Great Short-lived – whose zeal for God's House consumed Him. Make me Thy fuel, flame of God.

I have no doubt that that is what the Holy Spirit wants to do in our lives in these days. It is for such men and women God is looking.

---

1. Eric Alexander, 'We will give ourselves to prayer, and to the ministry of the Word' (p.129 in the present volume).
2. Ibid.

# KESWICK 1982 TAPES

List of tape numbers for addresses contained in this book.
The references follow the sequence of contents in the text.

**Bible Readings**
Rev Alec Motyer: 4 tapes 781, 782, 783, 784

Rev Philip Hacking: 4 tapes 811, 812, 813, 814

**Addresses**

| | |
|---|---:|
| Rev Eric Alexander | 780 |
| Dr Ronald Dunn | 785 |
| Rev Tom Houston | 797 |
| Rev Harry Kilbride | 817 |
| Rev Gilbert Kirby | 818 |
| Dr Ronald Dunn | 803 |
| Rev George Duncan | 816 |
| Rev Philip Hacking | 822 |
| Rev Tom Houston | 798 |
| Rev Alex Motyer | 799 |
| Rev Harry Kilbride | 823 |
| Rev George Duncan | 824 |
| Dr Ronald Dunn | 795 |
| Rev Eric Alexander | 805 |

These tapes can be obtained, together with a full list of
Keswick tapes, from:

> Anthony C Gill, Tape Secretary
> Keswick Convention Tape Library
> 13 Lismore Road
> Eastbourne
> East Sussex BN21 3BA